THE DISCOVERER OF INSULIN

Dr. Frederick G. Banting

Born: November 14, 1891

Died: February 21, 1941

When Frederick Banting discovered insulin, he gave millions of doomed diabetics the gift of life. He also found a preventive for the dread disease of silicosis, contributed to vital cancer research, pioneered in aviation medicine and flight psychology. He was honored for his services to science and humanity by the Nobel Prize for Medicine in 1923.

THE DISCOVERER OF INSULIN

Dr. Frederick G. Banting

by I. E. LEVINE

Julian Messner, Inc. *New York*

Published by Julian Messner, Inc.
8 West 40 Street, New York 18

Published simultaneously in Canada
by The Copp Clark Publishing Co. Limited

Fifth Printing 1962

Printed in the United States of America

Library of Congress Catalog Card No. 59-7013

For my wife Joy,
and my children David and Carol

Contents

• *CHAPTER ONE* •

"I want to cure, not comfort"

Spring had crept up on the peaceful Canadian countryside. It wove a bright green spell over the woods and fields of the modest Banting farmstead. The boy Fred and his two companions lay in the thick grass overlooking a small stream. Near by, curled up in slumber, was Collie, the Banting dog.

"When I grow up," Fred mused, "I think I'll be an explorer. There must be a thousand islands no one has ever found."

His cousin Fred Hipwell reached over to pluck a blade of timothy grass and put it between his teeth. "I want to be a doctor," he said. "Then we can go exploring together. In case someone is hurt, I can help him."

The third youngster was silent a moment. She was a tomboy named Jane, with dancing blue eyes and blonde disheveled hair. "Exploring is fun," she said at last. "But I'm a girl, and girls can't become explorers, can they?" There was a note of wistfulness in her voice.

"Not usually," Fred Banting explained gently. "But we'll be different. We'll take you along as a cook and nurse."

The girl's pretty freckled face brightened at thus being reassured. All of a sudden, she leaped up. "Let's go to Scout

Island and look for flint heads!" she shouted merrily. And before the boys could jump to their feet Jane was off like a shot, scampering down the riverbank with the now wide-awake Collie yipping at her heels.

It was on such spring days that Fred Banting truly loved his father's farm near Alliston, Ontario. For a nine-year-old boy a farm was a magic world to be explored. There were the fields and streams and a thousand and one places to look for buried treasure. But best of all was Scout Island, in the middle of the meandering Boyne River, where Fred and Cousin Fred Hipwell and Jane, their closest playmate, could play at being pirates or Indians or a hundred other games.

Islands held a curious fascination for Fred Banting. He never tired of daydreaming about them. Years later he was to perform a scientific miracle by exploring a group of magic islands in the living body. In those later times, the boyhood dreams of unknown islands were to come back to him out of half-forgotten memories and bring a smile to his lips.

But spring on a farm in 1900 was a wondrous time for another reason, too. It was the season of Nature's blessings, when the cows and pigs and other beasts gave birth to their young. For a sensitive, inquisitive boy like Fred, the miracle of life was an ever-unfolding panorama he never grew tired of watching.

He had a way with animals. The reason was not hard to find. He was gifted with a gentle, sympathetic nature that he seemed to come by naturally. In addition, he had learned from his father William Banting, a deeply religious man, that God demands a respect for all living things, whether human or animal.

Fred could remember the many times his father had sat up half the night with a foaling mare or a sick cow. His great gnarled hands were tender as a woman's as he soothed the suffering beasts and tried to ease their pain. If the animal died, he would come in from the barn silently, trying to keep his grief to himself. Yet it was quite obvious to the whole Banting family that he had suffered a blow not unlike that of losing a dear and trusted friend.

At such times, Margaret, Fred's mother, a small, lively woman with the dry humor and quiet fortitude of her Scottish forebears, would remind her husband of an ancient admonition. "The good Lord does not wish us to weep too long for those who have gone yonder," she would say. "He wants us to conserve our strength so that we may care for the living around us."

While Fred loved all animals, his favorites were the dogs. Never was the Banting farm without a dog. True, there were cats which lorded over the barns and feasted on the field mice. But the dogs were the important nonhuman members of the large Banting family and had a steadfast place in the household.

There had been several generations of dogs, but best of all was Collie, a tongue-wagging, frisking, mischievous beast that liked nothing better than to torment the slinking cat who bossed the barnyard. In spite of his name, Collie's family tree was as indeterminate as his loyalty to the family was unwavering. He was Fred's inseparable companion, playing an important role in the exciting games his young master devised together with Cousin Fred and Jane. When Fred mounted Betsy, the clumpy farm horse, and galloped off toward the small brick schoolhouse in Alliston two miles away, Collie would bid them good-by by trotting at the mare's heels, barking and cavorting like a clown until they passed the farm gate. Then he would turn back to keep Mrs. Banting company until the boy returned in the afternoon.

William Banting, Fred's father, was one of the many farmers who had helped build up Canada toward the end of the last century. God fearing, hard working, he combined a deep religious fervor with a simple and practical wisdom and goodness. These qualities he tried to communicate to his children.

Of English stock, John Banting, William's father, had been born in the north of Ireland. He had married and fathered a large family. Then, inspired by the stories of the rich and fertile lands in the provinces across the seas, he had moved to Canada about the middle of the last century. His son William became a farmer like his father. He loved the soil and respected it as the source of all life. To him, it was the property of God, and so it was holy. His religious nature impelled him to be active in the Methodist church. He became a trustee of the church and was so devoted to its tenets and moral values that fellow farmers and friends regarded him with the deep respect accorded a minister. Indeed, in later years, it was often mistakenly said that Fred's father was a minister!

William struck out on his own. On January 28, 1879, he wed saucy and pretty Margaret Grant, daughter of Sarah Ann Squire and Alexander Grant, both of whom were of Scottish blood.

Margaret had five children—Nelson, Thompson, Kenneth, Esther and Frederick. There was a gap of four years between Esther and Fred, the youngest. Frederick Grant

Banting was born on November 14, 1891, in the downstairs front bedroom of the white frame farmhouse near Alliston.

For a time before Fred's birth, William Banting had worked a farm near Beeton. He had wondered whether he should strike out for the unsettled Canadian West and make his stake. Land was practically free for the asking, but the hardships were almost insurmountable. It meant plunging his wife and children and life's savings into the wilderness, far away from civilization, schools, neighbors and comforts. For himself, William would have undertaken this challenge, but he wrestled with his conscience and decided he could not subject his growing family to such an ordeal. Instead, he decided to remain in Ontario and took a farmstead in Essa Township, hard by the town of Alliston.

Had William followed his first inclination and moved his vigor and ambition and family to the Far West, there is little doubt that Fate would not have caused Fred to join the ranks of the titans of the twentieth century who have done so much to conquer disease. For the chances are that he would not have gone to college and to medical school.

William and Margaret raised their family with a simple rustic wisdom. William was not only a church trustee, he was a teacher in the Sunday school and a member of the choir. He encouraged his children to love music, respect religion and seek knowledge. The Bantings were tolerant, broad minded and industrious. They instilled in their offspring the habit of perseverance and the love of hard work. It was a quality young Fred carried with him all the days of his life. It was one of the main reasons he was able to succeed in the great tasks he set for himself in later years.

As a boy, Fred did his share of the chores. He helped in the planting of the crops and the breeding of the animals.

He stirred the huge black pot of melted animal fat and watched spellbound as it underwent the mysterious chemical process that would turn it into soft soap. And always he asked questions, endless questions, for he was innately curious about all things he did not understand.

With his brothers he shared a natural aptitude for drawing. He was always to be seen sketching scenes about the farm. Later, he tried his hand at cartoons which he framed and gave as presents to the other members of the family. His first oil painting was a gift to Thompson, his oldest brother.

Books also absorbed his attention. He loved to read, and he especially enjoyed hearing his parents read aloud. Later on, he was to say that some of his happiest childhood memories were those of his father and mother taking turns at reading aloud to each other while he listened in rapt attention.

Fred was popular with his schoolmates. Although he was not a brilliant student, he was persistent and plucky and soon earned a reputation for sticking to a job until it was done. This doggedness was an attribute he had learned from his parents, and it earned him the respect of grownups as well as of his friends.

He was a powerful swimmer and once saved a friend from drowning. Although not a natural athlete, he made up in persistence what he lacked in inborn ability. At one time he made up his mind to become a marathon runner. So for months he could be seen every afternoon trotting along the country roads, training for the rugged sport. He also learned to play a good game of soccer and hockey and was a member of the Alliston High School baseball team the year it won the league championship.

Once, while coming home from school, he paused to watch two carpenters shingling the edge of a roof. Suddenly, the scaffolding broke and the workmen plummeted to the ground. They seemed to be badly injured, so Fred ran for the doctor. He was fascinated by the gentle and skillful way the physician examined and bound up their bruised and broken limbs.

Perhaps Cousin Fred has the right idea, he thought later. Maybe it would be a good thing to be a doctor and stop pain and suffering. Thereafter, he and Jane and Cousin Fred, whose father was the town druggist, spent a good deal of time in the back of the drugstore in a newly discovered world of test tubes and brightly colored medicines which were stored in large, tightly corked bottles.

Fred Banting was fourteen when Jane, who was the same age, suddenly took ill. One moment she had been gay and laughing, and the next a terrible change had come over her, it seemed. She was tired all the time and began to lose weight. She developed a constant craving for food and drink; and though she ate and drank a great deal she was always ravenously hungry and thirsty. But the more she ate, the more emaciated she became. In a matter of months, her once-sturdy young body was like that of a skeleton. Her legs grew thin and her face gaunt. Her eyes, once so lively and bright, were now sad and dull. She no longer wanted to jump or run or play with her friends.

Fred did not like to talk about Jane, even to his parents. It was as if he feared that talking about her dreadful illness might, in some mystical way, make her condition worse. But each night in the privacy of his own room he offered up a silent prayer for her to get well.

Her death came as a shock, although during the months

of her illness Fred had understood that she was suffering from a grave malady. He sensed this from the hushed tones of his parents and the other grownups when they spoke of her. Yet this knowledge did not lessen the shock.

It was the dreadful finality of Jane's death that confused and bothered him. He began to brood. He asked himself why people die and why the doctor, with all his books and medicines, had not been able to cure her. Illness always touched him deeply. Now it was as if he felt a sense of guilt because Death had claimed Jane, not him. Death was something he could not comprehend. It happened to old people, not to the young. And when it did strike the young, was it not because they had done something wrong? Had he not done the same things Jane had done—run through the same fields, played the same games, talked about the same things? These were good things, happy things. Yet Jane had been punished in a terrible way. Why had he not been punished, too?

Diabetes was the name the physician had given to Jane's illness. It was a mysterious illness that killed hundreds of thousands of people each year. He learned from Cousin Fred who knew about such things, that in the case of children it was even more swift and deadly than for adults.

During the days before Jane's funeral Fred did not show up for soccer practice behind the school. He avoided his classmates because he did not wish to talk about sports and other unimportant things. It would not be fair to Jane's memory, he felt. Instead, he came home right after school and called for Collie, who came tumbling out of his buffalo-skin doghouse under the cherry tree behind the farmhouse. Together, they would take long walks along the bank of the Boyne, visiting the secret places he and Cousin Fred and Jane had explored a thousand times.

One day he came home from school to find his father waiting in the kitchen. The huge man with the gentle eyes placed a work-toughened arm around his son's shoulder.

"Would you walk with me to the north pasture fence, boy?" he said. "There's a break I've been meaning to mend."

William Banting and Fred walked slowly across the fields followed by the faithful Collie.

"There's a feeling I have that something is gnawing at you," the father said. "It's to do with poor Jane, I warrant. Do you care to confide in your father?"

Before he knew it, Fred's unhappiness was gushing out of him. It poured out in a maelstrom of words. Tears welled in his eyes. "Why did Jane have to die, Father?" he asked. "She was so good and so young. Why, she was no older than me. Is there a reason for it?"

"Aye, boy, there's a reason," William Banting replied solemnly. "But it's beyond my comprehension or that of any mortal man. You ask why Death strikes man and beast before their time, and I can't answer other than by saying it's God will. And as the Lord wills it, so we must accept. Isn't that what your mother says? She's a brave, wise woman, your mother. For she knows what we all should know, that at times there's nothing to be done but give comfort."

In truth, Fred had always known his parents to behave that way, unquestioning and serene in the face of tragedy, giving comfort to those in distress. They never complained. They took their strength and religion from the rich soil. For did it not give them sustenance, and thus was it not tangible proof of the eternal righteousness of the Lord?

The funeral took place on a chill autumn day. The pall-bearers were the boys and girls who had known Jane and loved her. Fred was one of them. All during the solemn service in the little Methodist church, he sat stiff and erect, trying to keep the tears from his eyes. He must not cry. Jane's family was grief stricken, and to see him cry would cause them greater anguish. No, he must give comfort. He must act like a man—like his father—strong and serene.

After the services, they carried the pitiful little casket to the churchyard, and there Jane was laid to rest forever.

That afternoon Fred walked in the fields with Collie. His family did not ask him where he was going. They sensed his profound grief and knew he must wrestle with it himself.

"Let the boy be," his father said softly after he left the farmhouse. "He's a baby no more. If he is to learn of Life, he must learn of Death."

Off through the woods and fields Fred tramped. It was gray and overcast and there was a chill in the air. The trees and grass were no longer green. The waters of the Boyne were sluggish, and it depressed him. It was there that he and Jane had learned to fish and swim. And in his mind's eye he could still see those glorious winter evenings when the river was frozen and he and Jane and the other girls and boys of the neighborhood and from town had gathered for a skating party. He recalled how cold and clear those moonlit nights were. They kindled a large, old-fashioned fire and the party sat around on logs. Before long, the fire melted through the ice and extinguished itself. The next morning, on the way to school, he saw the big hole in the ice.

It was hard to realize that Jane would never again go to a skating party or dive into the gentle waters on a hot summer's day. She was dead and buried in the town churchyard. Fred raised his eyes to the branches of a barren tree near by. A gust of wind plucked a withered brown leaf from a branch and carried it gently to the ground. Death, he thought, is a dried-up leaf falling from a tree in the autumn afternoon.

But why . . . why did Jane have to die so young? What was this terrible disease the doctor had not been able to cure? What caused diabetes?

At that precise moment Fred knew for certain what he must do. He must become a doctor. He must find out about the mysterious diseases that struck human beings and carried them away long before their time. He must make certain that boys and girls like Jane would have a chance to grow up healthy and happy.

What was it his father had said to him in these very fields a few days ago? "Sometimes, there's nothing to be done but give comfort. It's God's will."

God's will. Fred repeated the words aloud.

From somewhere in the recesses of his memory he recalled a sermon on a Sunday morning. The black-robed preacher had quoted from the Psalms. "The heaven, even the heavens, are the Lord's: but the earth hath he given to the children of men."

Did that not mean that disease and poverty and unhappiness on the earth were not God given? That God had given the earth to man so he could improve it and make it a better place in which to live?

Thus, Fred Banting, with a wisdom far beyond his fourteen years, had stumbled upon one of the deepest philosophical problems of the ages and had managed to find an answer for himself. He had found it as surely as men down through the ages had found it and applied it to their individual lives.

"Someday," Fred said to Collie, "I will become a doctor and find out why Jane died. I want to cure, not comfort."

Collie heard him. He stared up at his master and wagged his tail in quiet, canine understanding.

• *CHAPTER TWO* •

The Fateful Decision

The simple religion that pervaded the Banting household was uncomplicated by doubts, by questioning, by sophisticated cynicism.

Before William Banting went into the fields in the morning to grapple with the soil, he ate a hearty breakfast. After the meal, he read a portion of the Scriptures. Then the entire family knelt on the hard flooring and prayed. Following that, the Lord's Prayer was chanted in unison. To Fred, it was a beautiful moment and a splendid prelude to the day.

Finally, refreshed by food and prayer, the family scattered, each one to his own tasks.

Church attendance on Sunday was taken for granted, of course. Even as a child, Fred knew he was expected to sit quietly and be attentive. Sometimes this was hard to do. It was all very mysterious, and the deep, resonant voice of the preacher, while impressive, gave forth big words he did not understand. After a while, his eyes would roam to the stained-glass windows with their magnificent hues of red, blue, green and yellow. When the sun climbed higher, the light that fell through a blue-bordered window at the east side of the church bathed the platform, pulpit and the solemn, black-draped figure of the minister in a curious blue light.

But all in all it was a good, healthy background for a boy. His days were crowded. There was school. There were the morning chores. At harvest time, there was the excitement of loading wood to secure the house against the winter frost. There was the slaughtering of the fat pig and the rendering of the lard. There was berrypicking and homework. And of course there were the amusements, the reading and drawing and games, although since the death of Jane the games were not as much fun any more.

The change that had come over him since the fateful day of the funeral was apparent, even though many months had passed. But his mother knew that he must walk alone in this matter. She was a remarkable woman, Margaret Banting, a rare combination of warmth, piety and good humor. She tried hard not to show favoritism for Fred, but he was the youngest, after all, and needed her longer than the others. So with a quiet and alert wisdom, she stood by him always, ready to give a bit of her own strength if he needed it.

From the time Fred entered his teens, it had been the father's fondest hope that he would enter the ministry someday. It was an understandable dream for a man as deeply concerned with religion as William Banting was. Margaret agreed with her husband—up to a point. She would have been delighted if Fred were to choose the pulpit; but perhaps more so than her husband she realized that the decision would have to be his own.

At first, William Banting hinted at his ambition for his youngest son. But as time went on, he began to accept it as a matter of course. He would say, "I can think of no finer thing for a young man than to serve God. Aye, I will be proud to have my last child a minister."

Fred heard but said nothing. He did not want to hurt his father. Yet deep down he knew he must come to a decision one day and would have to inform his parents. But how to go about explaining to them that he wanted to become a doctor was a problem whose solution had escaped him until now.

During his final year in high school he told Cousin Fred that he had definitely made up his mind to become a physician. It had been Cousin Fred's ambition, too, for as long as he could remember. So they now had an additional bond to tie them closely together. What's more, Cousin Fred's father had also set the ministry as a goal for his son. When he and William Banting discussed it, they more or less took it for granted that the boys would enroll for the clergy together.

Thus, the two Freds were caught between the ambitions of their parents and their own inner longing to join the great crusade of science that had been launched throughout the world.

After all, this was the new century, the dawning of a new age. It was a momentous period because men in all the civilized nations were predicting an age of marvelous advances in the sciences and engineering. A shining civilization of peace, well-being and plenty made possible by new discoveries in chemistry, biology and physics was anticipated everywhere.

In Europe and America the Industrial Revolution had begun. The machine, harnessed to the new energies of steam, water power and electricity, was easing the lot of man and beginning to do much of his work for him. It was said that the time would come when man would no longer have to work at all, that marvelous machines of steel and iron would do it for him.

In all the nations there was a freshet of hope and expectation that all the ills and the hurts of a suffering humanity would eventually be over and done with.

In England, the Victorian age had ended with the death of the great queen who had been enthroned for sixty-four years.

Now, science and industry were uppermost in the minds of venturesome men. And medicine was an important part of this new age of science. There had been great strides in many areas. True, there were tuberculosis and pneumonia and diabetes and a host of other ills and plagues which made men fearful. But there were scientific geniuses like Louis Pasteur of France and Élie Metchnikoff, a Russian, who had opened the door to a new microscopic world of bacteria which promised to hold the answers to many of man's gravest health problems. And now medicines were being sought—and in some cases found—that would abate pain and cure maladies that up to now had been thought incurable.

So orators spoke glowingly of the great strides that would be made in the next hundred years. They spoke of the age of flight, when men would lift themselves into the outer reaches by mechanical power. They also predicted that men would plumb the depths of the seas; that men would discover new and untapped sources of energy. All this, these visionaries said, will come in our time and the time of our children. It was a prediction that was heard in France, in England, in Germany and, across the seas, in the United States and Canada.

The excitement of the great age caught the imagination of boys like Fred Banting and his cousin. They wanted to be part of the splendid crusade, to do things that would help mankind.

But to men like William Banting, the new era of science meant little. God fearing, hard working, he was more immediately concerned with the seasons and the crops. Fred understood this, and the last thing in the world he wanted was to break his father's heart. So for many months he wrestled with his conscience in an attempt to find an answer to his problem. Medicine or the clergy, which was it to be?

In the end, he thought he had found a perfect solution.

He had long ago given up his childhood ambition to become an explorer, but he never gave up his interest in adventure and exploration. He still liked to read books that told of exciting far-off places where civilization had not yet taken hold. One day, he read an account of David Livingstone who had ventured into darkest Africa and made many important discoveries that thrilled the world. When he finished the book, he knew he had found a way out of his dilemma.

He told his plan to Fred Hipwell. "We will become medical missionaries like Dr. Livingstone."

His cousin was delighted and agreed that they would pursue their careers together.

William Banting was dubious. "It's a worthy goal you've chosen, boy, I'll not deny that. But are you certain you know what you're getting into?" Doubtless, at that moment he was thinking of his own earlier ambition to stake a claim in the wilds of unsettled western Canada and of the dangers and hardships of such a life.

Mrs. Banting was even more concerned. She could see

her son in the sweltering tropics, hundreds of miles from the nearest civilized outpost, living among tribes of unfriendly head-hunting savages. It was a frightening prospect for a mother to have to face. Yet with her usual good sense, she knew it would be hopeless to try to talk him out of it. "If Fred is earnest about this plan of his," she told her husband, "we won't be able stop him. If he is not, then he will stop himself."

William Banting saw the wisdom of this. He agreed not to stand in the way. "If it's a medical missionary you're determined to be," he told Fred gently, "then I'll be proud for the world to know my son has dedicated himself to carrying God's word to those who need it the most."

In the fall of 1910, Freshmen Banting and Hipwell went down to Toronto together to register at Victoria College. It was an honorable old liberal arts institution that boasted among its alumni some of Canada's leading citizens.

After enrolling, the next step was to find living quarters. They obtained lodgings at 351 Huron Street, in Toronto. The rooms were modestly furnished, and for two college freshmen on a tight budget they were adequate.

From the very first, Fred Banting began to have doubts about his choice. For one thing, he found it hard to adjust to the social life expected of a college student. There were many pretty girls in the freshman class, but he was painfully shy and couldn't bring himself to ask for a date. Moreover, he had never learned to dance.

There was a sense of guilt, too. Fred knew that though he had chosen the ministry, his real ambition was to study medicine. So he couldn't quite shake off the feeling that he was enrolled under a pretext. His parents were sacrificing to send him through college, in a course he didn't really want. Therefore, he felt that to fritter his time away instead of studying would be unfair.

Actually, he had no cause to feel this way. His parents would have wanted him to reap all the rich benefits of college, including the opportunity to socialize with young men and women. But the human mind plays strange tricks when it is unhappy. And Fred was unhappy. He tried joining the college glee club. He forced himself to study extra hours in the hope it would stimulate his interest in the courses. But nothing he did could substitute for the spark of real interest that was missing. He did poorly in French. His Latin was disastrous.

Too, he found himself drifting away from the simple Methodism of his childhood. He continued to attend church services, out of habit and a desire to please his parents. But he grew more and more aware of the absence of the deep dedication to orthodox Methodism that is needed to become a clergyman. He wrote home weekly; as the months passed, however, the letters grew briefer and less enthusiastic. At home on the farm, Mrs. Banting read them with concern. She knew the time would soon come when Fred would be faced with a fateful choice.

During his sophomore year, in 1912, Fred came home to Alliston to spend the Easter holidays. By the time the brief vacation was at an end, he knew he would not return to Victoria College.

He visited the Reverend Dr. Addison, the kindly Methodist preacher, to tell him of his decision. "Are you certain it's not temporary doubt that besets you?" the clergyman asked. "There are times when the most dedicated grow unsure."

"No, Dr. Addison," Fred replied quietly. "I've thought

about it all this past year. It's not a temporary thing. I now know I will never be happy unless I become a doctor."

"Then you must follow as your conscience dictates and no one else's," Dr. Addison replied. "If you wish, I'll speak to your parents on your behalf."

But Fred gratefully declined the offer. "No," he said, "I thank you kindly, but it's something I must do for myself."

That night he broke the news. His parents did not chide him. They did not ask too many questions or try to sway him. Perhaps they had half expected it. In truth, it was enough for them that Fred had tried his best and failed. More they could not ask of him.

"It would be against the will of the Lord to go into the ministry when you don't hear the call," his father said simply.

Now the family was faced with a critical problem. The medical course was long and expensive. It would require many sacrifices. It would mean doing without many comforts. But William Banting was a realistic man. He was a farmer, and a farmer must be a realist. He was a man who took his obligations to his family seriously, so he began at once to plan how best to finance his son's medical education.

Not long afterward, Fred Hipwell followed his cousin's example and left Victoria College. Together, they decided to enroll in the University of Toronto Medical School in the fall.

For the rest of the school year, Fred Banting remained on the farm. He helped his father with the spring planting. He took care of the animals and made repairs on the barn and farmhouse. As summer drew to a close, there was the harvesting to be done and a hundred other chores. His muscles, grown soft and slack at college, became hard and sinewy once more. He was tanned and fit. And now, with the guilt and mental conflict resolved, his frame of mind was improved, too.

The medical school turned out to be a large, white brick building ornamented with Georgian porticoes and cupolas. Nevertheless, it was a businesslike structure well equipped with classrooms, lecture halls and laboratories. There was no mistaking its essential function—turning out well-trained physicians.

Fred Banting and his cousin arrived in Toronto and were registered in the "Meds Seventeen" class, which meant it would be graduated in 1917. The course was five years long. The first days were a confusing whirl of lectures, study periods and simple laboratory experiments. Like most of the students, Fred tried a number of boardinghouses before he found quarters that suited his needs, at 63 Gloucester Street, in the heart of the student section of town. It was the home of Catherine O'Neil, a widow, with two daughters. Fred shared his room with a friend from Alliston, Sam Graham, a mathematics student. Cousin Fred found rooms next door, at No. 65.

From the beginning, Fred Banting knew he had made the correct decision this time. He found the world of medicine fascinating. He soaked up physiology and anatomy like a sponge. Organic chemistry and bacteriology had a poetic appeal for him. He worked harder than ever before in his life, but he was not a plodder, working just to get good grades. His interest was deep and genuine, and marks meant little. In fact, they did not reflect his real brilliance as a student of medicine.

Once, some classmates asked the technician in the histology lab to prepare tissue sections. "Why don't you take a tip from Banting?" the assistant replied. "He's been preparing his own." The students were amazed to learn that this was so. Fred actually had been preparing sections of tissue for his own use, something unheard of in medical school tradition.

During those years, few medical students owned their own microscopes. By scrimping and saving, Fred managed to purchase a shiny, brass-finished Leitz. It cost fifty-seven dollars and fifty cents, a small fortune, but it was worth it. He soon became a good microscopist. He was forever pricking his finger to get blood samples. These he would place on slides and study with great care. It was not surprising that in a few months his knowledge of hematology—the study of blood—went far beyond the course requirements.

His interest in his medical studies gave him a healthier outlook in other areas, too. He began to show some interest in social activities. He was by no means a social lion, for he was still awkward and shy, but some of his classmates, including Cousin Fred, took him under their wing. He balked at first, but soon he took a mild pride in the swiftness with which he acquired the basic social graces. He invited girls on dates and began to attend the theater regularly and accept invitations to parties.

He became close friends with Mrs. O'Neil, his landlady. She enjoyed cooking the dishes that reminded him of home and took it upon herself to mend his shirts and sew on his buttons. The house itself was old fashioned and comfortable and reminded him of his own home. The front parlor had a green and white tiled fireplace, with handsome brass andirons. Mrs. O'Neil obtained a photograph of Fred and had it framed. She placed it on the mantel just above the fireplace and there it remained for many years.

Fred was deeply grateful for her kindnesses. In return, whenever he went home to Alliston on a week end, he came back staggering under a load of fresh vegetables from the farm. "All washed and lovely," Mrs. O'Neil would say, her face glowing with pleasure, as she picked the scrubbed carrots and bright red tomatoes from the basket.

Practical jokes have long been a tradition among medical students and Fred was no exception. He had a good sense of humor and liked to exercise it. One evening, when Sam Graham, his roommate, was at the library and Mrs. O'Neil was busy sewing in the parlor, he got an idea. He enlisted the landlady's daughter Anna as a coconspirator. They took a pillow and some old clothes and rigged Sam's bed to look as if someone were sleeping in it. They dimmed the light and went downstairs to the parlor to join Mrs. O'Neil, who hadn't the faintest idea what was in the wind.

When Sam came in, Fred's head was buried in a newspaper, and Anna, looking innocent, was busy with her needle and thread.

"Looks like a thaw outside," Sam remarked as he tramped upstairs to the room.

A moment later, he came barreling down. "There's someone asleep in my bed," he whispered hoarsely in a quavering voice. "What are we going to do?"

With Irish courage, the landlady seized a broom and marched grimly up the stairs while Fred and Anna swallowed hard to keep from exploding.

When she came down a minute later, wearing a sheepish grin, the plotters roared with laughter. The two victims soon joined in.

Fred made a name for himself in intramural athletics. He was a regular on the class Rugby team, playing the right scrim position. He was tough and lean, and there was no flabbiness in his one hundred and seventy pounds. The team won eighty-five per cent of its games. But he never tried out for the varsity because he felt it would take too much time from his studies.

The medical school faculty was a brilliant one. There were Alexander McPhedran, professor of medicine; A. B. McCallum, professor of biochemistry; James McKenzie, the pathology teacher, and J. Playfair McMurrich, who drummed into the students the importance of anatomy. All were eminent doctors. But the one Fred admired and respected the most was the famous surgeon Clarence Leslie Starr, who was then surgeon-in-chief of the Hospital for Sick Children. He became Fred's counselor and friend and it was a relationship that lasted for many years.

One day, Fred sat in on an unusually interesting lecture in biochemistry delivered by Professor McCallum. It proved to be prophetic. The professor told them about a fascinating group of "islands" located in an oblong-shaped gland of the digestive system called the pancreas. The tiny islands, known as the islands of Langerhans, were reputed to contain a "secret treasure"—the chemical machinery that burns up the sugar content of the human system. "Perhaps someday, someone in this very class will be the one to find this secret treasure," Dr. McCallum observed.

At times, Fred's devotion to the field he had chosen embarrassed his less energetic classmates. He put in long hours doing extra work. Often, he was more interested in experiments than in food. He would bolt a sandwich for lunch in order to dash back to the laboratory to test the reflexes of a rabbit. He devised many original experiments. He painted a nerve ganglion with nicotine and tickled the end of the nerve with a gentle electric current. Or he dissected the heart of a lab specimen and submerged it in special solutions to make it behave normally.

Eventually, under Dr. Starr's influence, he chose orthopedic surgery as his field of specialization. This is the branch of medicine that deals with the correction of deformities and the repair of injuries by surgical operations.

Starr had an affection for the earnest young medical student. He was a born teacher as well as a brilliant diagnostician and surgeon, and when he came across an unusual student his instincts as a teacher were aroused.

What was it about Fred Banting that evoked this special interest? Nothing you could pin down in a routine examination of record cards or grading sheets. Nor was it the long hours he gave to his studies, for many mediocre students did that simply to keep their heads above the academic waters. In fact, not even Dr. Starr himself could have given a clear explanation. Perhaps it was the ingenuity Fred showed in the laboratory or the refreshing and original way he had of approaching a routine study assignment. But whatever it was, some instinct, born of long experience, told Dr. Starr that here was a young man who would someday play an important role in modern medicine.

During Fred's third year in medical school the long shadow of World War I stretched across the seas and touched the lives of "Meds Seventeen." An Austrian archduke named Ferdinand was assassinated in the tiny Balkan kingdom of Serbia. Soon, all Europe was engaged in the grim business of death and destruction.

Fred and many of his classmates were overcome by a compelling sense of patriotism. They wanted to join the infantry as privates and go overseas. But older and wiser heads on the faculty restored sanity. Aghast at the thought of losing so many future doctors, they addressed the student body and convinced them that they could best serve Canada by finishing their studies first. They explained that patriotism is sometimes a more complex matter than shouldering a rifle and rushing off to the front lines.

Fred and the others decided to remain in school. But they joined a Canadian Officers' Training Corps organized at the university and drilled daily.

In the spring of 1915, he was assigned to work as a dresser at a military camp set up in Exhibition Park. One day a trainee reported to sick bay with a bad case of tonsillitis. There were not enough licensed doctors available, so medical student Banting was given special permission to perform the operation. Nervously, he leafed the pages of his standard textbook on minor operations and memorized every detail described in the section on tonsillectomies. Reassured, he strolled into the operating room trying his best to appear nonchalant and crisply professional. But inwardly, he could feel his heart thumping wildly. Several fellow students crowded around in a small perimeter and watched with awed envy as he bent over the patient with gleaming scalpel.

He knew the operation was a simple one and would take only a few minutes. Yet at the start it seemed like an eternity and it took all his will power to keep his hands from trembling. Step by step, he followed the standard surgical procedure, just as he had learned it. There were no complications. Good. Just a few moments more and the ordeal would be over. He could feel his self-confidence rising, and he knew now he was in complete control of the situation. Finally, it was done; the operation was over and it was a success. He stepped back, warmed by a sense of accomplishment.

Suddenly, he was startled out of his brief reverie by a familiar voice. "Well done, Banting." It was one of the professors who had quietly entered the room and observed the operation almost from the start.

He would remember those words proudly, wear them as a badge of honor. For it was the ultimate confirmation that in choosing the field of medicine he was on the road to fulfilling his own personal destiny.

War had a profound effect on the academic life of the medical school. The courses were accelerated and the terms shortened. The work and hours were harder and longer than ever. But Fred kept ahead of his class, although his grades still failed to show it.

"Meds Seventeen" was scheduled to graduate many months ahead of time—in December, 1916. On December 4, Fred was having lunch with the O'Neils when a classmate dropped by to inform him that final grades were ready in the medical school office.

Fred excused himself and rushed next door to tell Cousin Fred the news. Young Hipwell borrowed an automobile and loaded it with half a dozen students. Then off they roared, down the street toward the university. They dashed upstairs to the office of the secretary to the faculty to learn their fate.

They all passed.

A few minutes later, Fred and his cousin paused in front of the huge white building and turned to look at it. It was a brisk, cold winter's day, but high overhead a friendly sun was shining. It was not unlike one of the happy pre-

Christmas days Fred remembered from his childhood on the farm.

Finally, he turned to his cousin. "Congratulations, Doctor," he said.

The next day, he became Lieutenant Frederick Grant Banting of the Canadian Army Medical Corps.

• CHAPTER THREE •

Surgeon in Battle

As the train chugged out of Alliston, Fred sat in a forward car fighting off an intense sadness. He disliked farewells, because they were occasions when people displayed their emotions, and he tried to avoid emotional demonstrations when he could.

One of the reasons, perhaps, was his own inner sensitivity, for Fred Banting knew he was too easily given to moods, and dark moods made inroads on his time and emotions.

The last few minutes, when he had said good-by to his family—possibly for the last time—had not been easy. Everyone had tried to be gay and matter of fact, but it had not come off. In the end, his mother, usually so strong and self-reliant, wept silently. His father turned quickly to brush away an unshed tear. Sister Esther began to tell a joke, but her lips quivered so much she never finished it.

Fred himself tried to cover up his emotions by giving the appearance of being very military and unbending in his trim new officer's uniform. Now he regretted that he had not given way to his feelings a bit, if only as a sign to his mother of how he really felt. Yet he hoped that out of the closeness of their relationship, she would sense his true feelings.

Just before he boarded the train, his father had whispered a last word of encouragement. "You're a doctor now, boy, a healer. In a way you, too, carry the word of God. Carry it well."

Now, as he sat in the train, listening to the clickety-clack of the wheels as they slid over the steel rails, Fred thought of his father's words and silently vowed to justify his faith.

The last few days of his final leave had passed swiftly, too swiftly. And the weeks since his graduation from medical school had flown by. There had been no time for extensive officers' training or other peacetime frills. A war was on; doctors were desperately needed. Training had been cut to the bone. There had been the long weary days of infantry drill and the crowded evenings of lectures on administrative procedures.

Finally, he had been granted embarkation leave. On his way home, he had paused in Toronto to say good-by to Mrs. O'Neil and the girls. They had been delighted to see him and wept when he boarded the train for Alliston.

Back on the farm he had walked through the peaceful fields and along the banks of the Boyne. He strolled down the streets of town, waving to people he knew and bidding good-by to the shopkeepers who had known him since childhood. He had re-etched in his memory the stirrup-shaped sign over the door to Hipwell's Drugstore and the queer, triangular dormers of the tiny Windsor Hotel. On Paris Street, he had spent a good many minutes staring at the weather-beaten sign above Latimer's Carriage Works.

He had taken a sentimental journey through the land of his childhood in those last few days. And why not? He was twenty-six years old and headed overseas. The shops he visited and the friends he bade good-by had played a major part in his life up to now. If he were lucky enough to get back, he would see them again, of course. But if not, he wanted to carry their memory with him always.

In Quebec, he boarded a troopship, and within a few hours it weighed anchor and slipped silently out of the pier, heading for he didn't know where.

But if Lieutenant Banting expected to get to the front lines at breakneck speed, he was mistaken. He now learned something of the curious, roundabout way things are done in military organizations. At Campbellton, New Brunswick, the ship docked and the men were taken off. There would be a temporary delay, they were told. The delay stretched into weeks. What's more, since the Army had forgotten to send word of their arrival, arrangements to feed and house the soldiers had not been made. It was an emergency, and the good people of New Brunswick came to the rescue. They put up the soldiers in their own houses and fed them. It was an inspiring display of patriotism and neighborliness.

Saying good-by to his family and to Alliston had made Banting tense and eager to get to Europe. Like many of his fellow soldiers he wanted "to get this war over with and get back home." The stopover only made him more tense and impatient, although it gave him a chance to see a part of Canada he had never visited before.

Finally, they were marched back to the ship and got aboard. It was the real thing, this time. They headed for Europe in a calm, unruffled sea, although it was February. The journey proved to be uneventful. There were no submarines, and they made good time. They traveled by convoy.

Only once was there the promise of excitement. One of the ships struck a submerged object near the coast of England. There was a sharp jolt and the ship trembled. A rumor spread like wildfire that the waters were mined, but it turned out to be just that—a groundless rumor. The convoy continued safely to anchorage.

Banting was assigned to the Granville Canadian Special Hospital at Ramsgate, England. Shortly afterward, the hospital was moved to Buxton. He was happy with his assignment. The main task of the center was to treat orthopedic cases, and all sorts of cases came in from the front lines. It was a fine opportunity to learn surgery, his specialty, and as usual, he worked hard to improve his knowledge and technique. Soon, he developed a skill and speed in diagnosis and treatment of which he had never thought himself capable. In off-duty hours, he continued the independent experimenting he had begun in medical school. One of his superiors was so impressed by his eagerness that he arranged to supply him with laboratory specimens for dissection.

He also developed a hobby—and an extravagance: collecting rare china. He became enamored of English china and visited all the china shops within traveling distance. It took every spare cent of his lieutenant's pay, but he managed to collect some beautiful and unusual pieces.

But in spite of its many advantages, Banting soon grew discontented with his assignment He was eager to get into action. Like many of his fellows, he thought to himself: Let the older doctors take care of things here in England. I'm of fighting age and I should be in France, in battle.

His wish was not long in coming. He was transferred to the Thirteenth Field Ambulance Corps and soon shipping orders came through. The unit found itself crossing the English Channel, headed for the thick of the fighting.

Banting found that the life of a front-line surgeon was not easy. It was a rugged, continuing round of treating the wounded and easing the pain of the dying. The physical challenge was gruelling, but he was big, tough and in excellent shape, so he was a match for the endless hours of dressing wounds and performing minor miracles of battlefield surgery. The mental strain, however, was something else again.

He was by nature conscientious, always striving for perfection, and this was often impossible under front line conditions. The techniques he had learned in school would not do in the grimy surroundings of hastily set up dressing stations. He had to improvise, to use instruments and medicines that were not always the best for a particular job. He had to acquire the habit of depending on swift judgments and quick decisions. So although he got a great deal of surgical experience he would not have obtained in years of civilian practice, he worried a great deal. He was constantly beset by self-doubt, wondering if he had made the right decisions. This inner sensitivity took a lot out of him mentally. Even the knowledge that he was saving many lives did not comfort him. The patients he could not save were the ones who caused him grief and anguish. He constantly asked himself: Did that man die because I was at fault, or would he have died in any case? It was a terrible burden to live with, and he never quite grew hard enough to accept the death of a patient with the matter-of-factness that many of his less-sensitive fellow surgeons were able to develop.

His judgment was never a cause for doubt among Banting's superiors. They watched him work and learned to respect his common sense and courage. This was particularly true in the case of amputations. While some of the other young surgeons grew callous and indifferent and amputated a limb as an easy way out, Banting refused to sacrifice an arm or a leg unless he was certain it was absolutely necessary. In this respect he was considered daring, because he preferred to take some risk if it meant giving the patient a chance for a normal, happy life later on.

Since he was a commissioned officer, he was assigned an orderly. Kels was his name and he was a native of British Columbia. He was a shrewd, courageous soldier and hard as nails. But he developed a respect and affection for Banting that was unusual in an officer-enlisted man relationship. In return, Fred learned to hold him in great esteem.

Kels had one skill that virtually amounted to genius—he always managed to dig up items no one else could find. Cigarettes, soap, chocolate—name it and Kels could get it, even if it was out of supply. It was a characteristic the other soldiers envied.

He was also an expert at dreaming up substitutes and contriving makeshift equipment. In later years, one of Banting's favorite subjects of conversation was Kels and some of the amazing things he did.

Once, Kels surprised Fred by serving mushrooms with the regular bully beef ration. No one in the unit had seen a mushroom for months, and pressed for an explanation, the orderly explained that he had gone into the battle area and picked the delicacy under the very noses of the enemy.

Another time, the unit moved to a new site which had been recently occupied by the Germans. Water was desperately needed. Finally, a well was located. But Banting refused to allow his men to use it. "It may be poisoned," he warned. "The enemy has done that to the other wells, you know."

Kels disappeared for a short time. When he returned, he said, "I think you'll find the well is all right, sir."

"How do you know?" Banting asked suspiciously.

"Because they said it was all right," the orderly said, brandishing a pistol in the direction of three prisoners of war lined up near by.

"Maybe they're lying," Banting insisted.

"I doubt it, sir," Kels retorted calmly. "After they told me the water wasn't poisoned, I decided to make sure. So I made every one of them drink it."

Banting and his orderly made an unusual pair, and their exploits became legendary in the Thirteenth Field Ambulance.

One afternoon, the two of them came upon an "abandoned" enemy dugout in a forward area.

"What shall we do, Lieutenant?" Kels asked. "There may be jerries hiding in there."

"Why, then we'll flush them out," Banting replied coolly. "Keep me covered."

With Kels remaining outside, armed with a rifle, the surgeon nonchalantly descended into the dugout. There, huddled together, were three fully armed enemy soldiers!

Fred sized up the situation at once. "Drop your guns!" he barked in improvised German. "The dugout is surrounded. I have a whole machine gun company outside ready to start shooting!"

The terrified Germans dropped their rifles and raised their hands high in token of surrender. *"Kamerad!"* they pleaded. "Do not let them shoot us!"

They marched out of the dugout to face an amazed Kels. Later, Banting had to make a personal report of the incident to his commanding officer.

"How were you armed when you 'assaulted' that dugout?" the incredulous major asked.

"With my swagger stick, sir," Fred replied.

Not long afterward he was promoted to captain and assigned temporarily to the Forty-fourth Battalion, about to go into battle. As the battalion surged forward in a harrowing attack mission, Banting moved ahead with a small medical detail. Enemy shells were exploding everywhere, and showers of dirt mushroomed about them. Men were falling on all sides. The spine-chilling screams of the wounded added to the confusion. But in spite of it, Banting and his medical corpsmen succeeded in setting up the first dressing station in the battle area.

The casualties were numerous, and the detail was unable to care for them all. Banting hunted around until he found a captured German medical detail. He ordered the prisoners to help, but one German doctor protested. The Canadian tried to reason with the enemy officer, but it did no good. Finally, Banting lost his temper.

"Your own people are among the wounded," he said through clenched teeth. "I order you, not as a prisoner of war, but as a doctor who has taken an oath to help humanity."

The German changed his mind, and side by side, the Canadians and Germans worked around the clock. Hundreds of wounded were given first aid and cleared for shipment to rear area stations and hospitals. Scores of lives were saved. Banting was everywhere, supervising the entire operation. Although he was on the verge of physical exhaustion, he refused to rest, in spite of the pleadings of his men. He kept going until the battle was over and every wounded man was cared for.

For his remarkable feat, Banting was recommended for the Military Cross by the Forty-fourth Battalion. But somewhere along the line, the papers were lost or mislaid. The decoration did not come through at that time.

Now he was sent to rejoin the Thirteenth Field Ambulance, and once again he found himself in the thick of battle. All day and all night the constant roar of enemy guns kept the Canadians tense and on guard. They couldn't sleep or relax even for a moment. When a shell came whistling close by, they flattened themselves in the dirt. Soon the entire unit was suffering from a bad case of nerves.

One day, Major L. C. Palmer, who commanded the unit, came across an amazing sight. Captain Banting was sitting calmly in a trench, reading an anatomy manual, apparently oblivious to the roar of the big guns. When the story got out, the other men in the unit roared with laughter. It was the first relaxing moment they had had in many days.

Autumn, 1918. The big Allied push began, British, Canadian and American forces were poised to strike at the heart of the German resistance. By the end of September, the attack had begun, and the Second Battle of Cambrai was on. It proved to be one of the crucial actions of the war.

On September 28, stretcher bearers from Major Palmer's and Captain Banting's unit were assigned to clear the wounded from the forward area. The two officers were busy at the dressing station giving first aid to the wounded brought in by horse ambulance and wheeled stretchers from the advanced positions. The station had been set up in a partially wrecked barn, near an old farmhouse where German prisoners were being held. High above the barnyard, shells from distant enemy guns were erupting like deadly, blossoming flowers.

As Banting was bandaging the leg of a wounded corporal, he paused to glance out of the door of the barn. He saw a

German prisoner, a major, standing on the farmhouse steps a few yards away, calmly smoking a cigarette. Why doesn't that fool get back in the house, he thought. He'll get himself killed.

A moment later, the German major was lying in the blood-soaked dirt of the barnyard, killed instantly by a piece of shrapnel. Banting had sunk to his knees, his forearm almost split in two by a steel fragment from the same shell.

The first thing he remembered was that he had not heard the shell burst that got him. Afterward, he remembered thinking, too, that it must have been a whiz-bang, a type of shell devised by the Germans that did not give a warning whistle before exploding.

The fragment that penetrated Fred's arm had gone deep enough to sever an artery. Almost immediately, Major Palmer was at his side, helping him to his feet. The major took him to the shelter of a brick wall and examined the bloodstained arm. He ripped the sleeve of the uniform and applied a tourniquet to stop the bleeding. Then he carefully removed the piece of shrapnel and bandaged the forearm.

"There's an ambulance waiting," he told his junior officer. "Get into it. It's back to the rear lines for you."

"It's nothing, just a scratch," Banting protested. "Don't send me back. I'll be all right. After all, you're shorthanded here, sir."

"Nothing doing," Major Palmer insisted. "There's a bad wound . . ."

At that moment, a runner came up with a message for the major to proceed immediately to the forward battle area to set up a new dressing station. He looked at Banting and hesitated. The captain was the only remaining officer—he knew that. But he was also in a state of shock, haggard from overwork, pale from the loss of blood.

Palmer made up his mind. "Get into the ambulance," he said firmly. "The sergeants can do the dressings," and he left for the forward area.

He returned seventeen hours later to find Banting still at the first-aid station, still on his feet, still dressing wounds.

He was furious. "I thought I told you to get out of here!" the major shouted. "You disobeyed a direct order. Are you out of your mind?"

"But there was no one else to take charge here," Banting protested wearily.

"The sergeants could have done it, I told you that," Palmer said more gently. "Why, you should be in a hospital this very minute. Are you trying to kill yourself?" It was obvious that his initial anger was now tempered by the magnificent courage of the young captain.

Once more he ordered Banting into an ambulance, but this time he went along to make sure the order was obeyed. Fred climbed into the front seat beside the driver without further protest. When the vehicle jolted off through the darkness, the major returned to the dressing station. It was four in the morning. Things were fairly quiet. He helped the sergeants finish dressing the wounded who were waiting to be moved out to the rear area. Then, bone tired, he sat down at a packing case that served him as a desk and wrote out a recommendation that Frederick Grant Banting, Captain, Canadian Army Medical Corps, be awarded the Military Cross.

It was the second time Banting had been put in to receive the decoration, one of Canada's highest military honors.

This time, the recommendation reached London and was approved.

Meanwhile, the heavily loaded ambulance carrying Banting bounced over the shell-pocked road. He kept falling into fitful, feverish sleep only to be awakened by the jolting and the throbbing pain in his right forearm. In spite of the jarring, the wound did not hemmorhage—until the ambulance pulled into the clearing station. Then it began to bleed profusely, and the wounded surgeon lapsed into merciful unconsciousness.

He was carried into the station and placed on a cot. A medical officer stopped the bleeding and injected morphine to relieve the pain, then dressed the wound with fresh bandages. Through it all, Banting slept. . .

He was clearheaded when he awoke. The doctor informed him he would most likely be evacuated to England. Fred protested. "It's not serious. I'll be up and around shortly. Besides, my unit needs me."

The doctor shot him a look that clearly indicated he thought his patient was delirious or insane, then left.

Before long, Banting had a visitor. It was Kels. The orderly slipped him a small package containing a slice of angel food cake one of the enlisted men had received in a parcel and had sent along to "the captain." It was the first food he had eaten in nearly twenty-four hours.

A short time later, Captain Banting was transferred to another hospital. They wheeled him into an operating room, administered an anesthetic and scraped the wound clean.

When he awoke again he was conscious of someone moving around near by in the semidarkness. Gentle hands tucked the blanket tightly about him. He assumed it was a nurse and didn't even bother to open his eyes. He groped for a cigarette with his left hand. The unseen "nurse" placed one between his lips and touched a match to it. He inhaled deeply, gratefully.

"Are you comfortable now, sir?" a familiar voice whispered. "You seemed to be cold a few moments ago so I got an extra blanket."

Kels! Banting forced himself to open his eyes. It was indeed Kels. Who else? But how had the orderly discovered what hospital he'd been transferred to? Suddenly, there was the rustling of a starched uniform as a nurse approached. Kels seemed to melt into thin air. As soon as she went away, he reappeared, and stayed close by for the next few days.

When Banting was carried to the ambulance train for evacuation to the coast, there was Kels. He arranged for the captain to be in a compartment with a window, so he could watch the passing scenery. As the train pulled out, Kels was still with Banting, and no one bothered to ask questions. He stayed on all the way to Calais, performing all sorts of minor miracles such as finding hot water for shaving and even an English newspaper for Banting to read.

The wounded surgeon knew his orderly must have been AWOL, but when he asked him about it, Kels turned the question aside with an evasive smile. "Don't bother your head about it, sir," he said. "Just leave it to old Kels."

At Calais, they parted. "This is good-by, Captain," the orderly said with a sorrowful grin. "I'm afraid I'd better not try the Channel." Banting smiled gratefully and awkwardly shook Kels's hand with his left, the right being in a sling around his neck.

The soldier disappeared—for the last time. Later, Fred learned that in some mysterious fashion Kels had managed to rejoin the unit the next morning—without even being missed!

In England, Banting was sent to a general hospital in Manchester. From there, he was shipped to his old station, the Special Hospital at Buxton, this time as a patient. His arm had become infected.

At Buxton, there was hurried consultation among the surgeons. One of them, a young lieutenant, fresh overseas, finally came to Banting with the bad news.

"Im sorry, Captain, but I think we'll have to amputate. The arm looks very bad." The tone was flat, colorless, almost matter of fact.

Fred was stunned. He thought of the scores of time he had been faced with the same decision, playing God, so to speak—and now the situation was reversed; now *he* was the patient. It was a curious, mixed-up world, all right, this world of war and destruction and death.

He looked down at his bandaged right arm. He saw the hands and fingers of a doctor, a surgeon. The hands of a surgeon are his whole life. Without them he ceases to be a surgeon, ceases to exist. Yet there was a fresh-water lieutenant blithely ordering him to lose his right arm, in the same tone of voice he might use to tell him the time of day.

"No," Banting said at long last. "You are not to amputate. I won't let you. I've seen the wound. It will be all right. It will be all right, you'll see. I'll treat it myself." It was a decision not unlike the other times when he had weighed the chances of saving a patient's limb against the risk to the patient's life. But this time there was another factor to be considered, this time it was his own arm and his own life that were hanging in the balance.

Clearly, the lieutenant was confused. He had never had a

patient tell him he didn't know what he was talking about. This, however, was no ordinary patient. This was a captain, an officer of superior rank—a wounded officer, it was true—but nevertheless a medical officer like himself. It was a most unusual situation, one he had never come up against, and quite frankly he didn't know how to handle it.

He tried to reason with the captain, and this time there was a new note of respect in his voice. "But sir . . ." he began.

Banting raised himself painfully on his left elbow. "You heard me!" he said in a rising voice. "You're to leave the arm alone, do you hear? I know what I'm doing." His lean, battle-hardened features were set in a stubborn frown.

It was clear he was getting angry, and the young lieutenant beat a strategic retreat.

The doctors did not amputate.

• *CHAPTER FOUR* •

The Road Back

The war was over. For Captain Banting it had ended the moment he had been struck by the jagged shell splinter at Cambrai. But now it was over for all of them—the living and whole limbed as well as the maimed.

Fred was recuperating at Buxton when the Armistice was declared. His arm healed slowly and painfully. At times the terrible aching kept him awake most of the night, and the dawn found him drawn and white, his body bathed in sweat. But in the end he recovered, to the amazement of the other surgeons. His own stubborn determination was the key factor, and eventually the experience left him with nothing worse than a painful memory and a deep, ugly scar.

When he was shipped home from overseas duty early in 1919 he was assigned to the Christie Street Hospital in Toronto to await his army retirement. It was a welcome interlude, for it gave him time to think about his future. At the hospital he met Marion Robertson, a pretty young technician who was doing electrotherapy work. They were attracted to each other at once, but Banting's rigid sense of honesty kept the relationship from developing into anything serious. He felt it would be unfair to the girl to encourage a romantic attachment before he was settled in civilian life and could think about marriage.

More than anything else, he needed time to readjust. The Canada to which he had returned was a country he hardly knew. Physically, of course, it was unchanged. It was still a young, vigorous land burgeoning with new industries and opportunities, many of them stimulated by the war. His parents' farm near Alliston was the same as it always had been. And his parents themselves had not really changed, although they were grayer and more aged—his father was nearing seventy. But in spite of the surface similarities, he sensed a change in the Canadian people themselves. There was a new restlessness all about him—almost a lack of purpose. It was as if the war had uprooted the old and familiar virtues, the old sense of security that gave people a common purpose, and left nothing in its place. He had read somewhere that all wars affect nations in this way.

While the fighting was going on, everyone was united in common effort, motivated by a clear, attainable goal—military victory. But when the war was over, the sense of direction was momentarily lost, and no one knew quite where he wanted to go. "Normalcy" was the cry he heard quite often now. "Let's forget about the war and get back to normalcy." He soon learned that this attitude was prevalent in other countries, too, yet he couldn't help feeling that this frenzied desire of people to return to "normalcy" was a mirage. The war had wrought many changes, after all. Not only had it killed and maimed; it had also destroyed many of the illusions people had once held. Science and industry had improved travel and communications and made the world smaller. Now, like it or not, all the nations of the earth were tied up in a common destiny. If the war had shown anything, it had proved that when a few nations begin to fight each other, everyone else is soon drawn into the battle. Did this not mean that every man has a responsibility to everyone else? That every human being was in a very real sense "his brother's keeper," just as he had heard his father say so often when he was a child?

What disturbed Fred greatly was that few seemed to feel this way. Most of the people seemed to be concerned wholly with their own individual needs, with no time or inclination to think about others. And yet was it the others who were out of step with the new world that had been shaped, or was it he, Fred Banting, who was out of tune with things?

Here he was, twenty-eight years old and a licensed physician who had seen nothing but war for two years. On the battlefields he had seen man's cruelty and heroism in their most naked form. Now he was transported back to a peacetime existence where the very qualities that were so prized in a soldier were held in contempt. In war, soldiers were encouraged to kill the enemy but to be concerned for the welfare of their fellows. In peace, just the opposite was true: Killing was abhorred but the individual was encouraged to think only of himself.

The more he thought about it, the more moody he became. From past experience, Banting knew that when a blue spell came upon him the quickest cure was to plunge himself into hard work. He did this now. As soon as he retired from the Army he accepted an appointment to work as a resident physician at the Sick Children's Hospital in Toronto under Dr. Starr, his beloved professor. What's more, he rented his old quarters at 63 Gloucester Street. Mrs. O'Neil was delighted and treated him like a prodigal son who had returned home. "When you're in Toronto, this is your home," she told him in no-nonsense tones. "I won't stand for your staying anywhere else, eating food your stomach's not used to. And I know your mother, bless her, wouldn't have it, either."

During the next year, Banting worked hard, learning more about orthopedic surgery, particularly on children. Dr. Starr was delighted at the skill he had developed in the Army, but not surprised. After all, hadn't Fred Banting been his most conscientious student at medical school?

"For all its painful memories," he told the youthful resident physician, "your war experience has made a surgeon out of you."

All sorts of cases came through the wards of the hospital. Soon, Banting found himself specializing in the mechanical correction of childhood deformities such as crooked backs, clubfeet and twisted and spastic limbs. He had always been fond of children, and now he found that the more hideous the deformity, the greater was his sympathy and affection for the tiny patient. With adults, a trace of his boyhood shyness remained, but with youngsters he was warm and completely at ease.

When he wasn't treating the little boys and girls in his wards, he was busy telling them stories and jokes. He had a wry sense of humor the children loved. And while he told them all sorts of wonderful tales, he would peer owlishly through his thin-rimmed spectacles. The parents who came during visiting hours thought of him as tight lipped and reserved. Consequently they were amazed when their youngsters referred to him as "Uncle Doctor Fred."

Banting usually did not refer to his own war wound when talking with grownups. But with the children, particularly those who were self-conscious about their afflictions, he rolled up the right sleeve of his white physician's jacket and showed them his scar. "See," he said, "even Uncle Doctor Fred has a bad hurt. But it's only the outside. It has nothing to do with what you are on the inside. And that's the important thing, being a good person on the inside."

Dr. Bruce Robertson, a famous Canadian physician, was doing pioneer work in blood transfusions at the Sick Children's Hospital at this time. The technique was still in its infancy and donors were scarce. So in addition to his regular duties Banting volunteered to give blood. On several occasions he dashed to the hospital during his rare off-duty hours to donate blood to critically ill children.

Mrs. O'Neil scarcely saw him during those months. He was at the hospital almost around the clock, coming back to the house only to gulp down a sandwich or to change his clothes. It soon reached the point where Dr. Starr himself was forced to order the resident to leave the hospital and get some rest.

Occasionally, Fred managed to get home to Alliston for a week end. But even in the relaxed atmosphere of the farm he found it hard to stop worrying about the welfare of his young patients.

"You're a conscientious lad," his father would say. "It's the price one pays to be a good physician, I warrant, and for that I'm proud. I do know this—if ever I'm in need of a doctor, which thank the Good Lord I'm not now, I'd rather have one like yourself than one that's in it for the glory and not much more."

When the summer of 1920 rolled around, Banting knew he must start thinking about hanging up a shingle as a private practitioner. He thought vaguely of remaining in Toronto. Then one day he ran into Dr. W. P. Tew, a classmate from medical school. Tew advised him to think about going to London, the second largest city in western Ontario.

"There is much greater opportunity in London than in Toronto," he explained, "especially for fellows like us who are just starting out. At least that's my thinking for what it's worth. I'm opening an office there in August."

Tew also pointed out that London had a fine medical school, the medical school of the University of Western Ontario. At the moment it was located in cramped, antiquated quarters and didn't have adequate laboratory space, but a beautiful new building was being completed which would provide elaborate, up-to-date facilities.

To Banting this constituted a powerful argument. For it meant he would be able to keep up with the latest medical developments at all times by having access to the school's medical library. And perhaps he could even arrange to use the laboratories if he felt like doing research in his spare time, a field he had been so interested in as a medical student.

He asked Dr. Starr for advice. The professor was enthusiastic. "There's not a doubt in my mind that you're ready to go into practice," he declared. "London might not be a bad place to start. You'll be sorely missed here at the hospital, of course. But it would be selfish of me to prevail on you to stay."

There was a note of sadness in the great surgeon's voice. The two were more than pupil and teacher. They were friends, bound together by mutual ties of understanding and loyalty. Just as Starr would miss him, Banting would miss his teacher's wise counsel and steadfast encouragement.

On the first day of July, Dr. Frederick Banting, orthopedic surgeon, rattled into London behind the wheel of a battered old Ford he had picked up in Toronto. Piled into the back seat were three ancient suitcases containing all his worldly possessions. As the car wheezed up a busy thoroughfare, he felt alone and friendless. For a brief moment, in fact, he almost regretted his decision. London was a big, bustling town. He was a stranger here. Would it prove too formidable for a farm boy from Alliston about to start out on a major phase in his medical career?

Banting pulled over to the curb, extracted a cigarette from a half-empty pack on the seat beside him and lighted it while pondering his next move. Finally, he climbed out of the car and entered a small tobacconist's shop where he made a telephone call. There was no mistaking the familiar voice on the other end. It was his old roommate from Mrs. O'Neil's boardinghouse, Sam Graham. Earlier Fred had written his friend to tell him of his plans for practicing in London.

Now Sam insisted Fred drive out to his house for dinner. Banting accepted eagerly. He was tired and hungry from the long drive, but most of all he wanted to see a friendly face.

When he drove up the quiet tree-lined street and parked in front of the house, Sam was waiting at the gate. He was older and heavier now but he had not lost his infectious, good-natured grin. He had done well, for he was now the principal of a London collegiate school. They slapped each other on the back delightedly and strolled into the house arm in arm. Already Fred felt a renewed sense of confidence. That evening after dinner they sat in the parlor and spoke about the old days at Mrs. O'Neil's, including the hilarious incident of the stuffed bed.

With a loan from his father for a down payment, Banting

soon arranged to buy a house from a shoe merchant named Rowland Hill. It was a large white-brick residence at 442 Adelaide Street North. He agreed to let Hill continue to live there for a year, until his new home would be built. But Banting was to have a bedroom and the use of the front parlor for an office.

One morning a large van pulled up in front of the house and the driver and his helper unloaded some brand-new office furniture—a gift from his parents! The pieces were not pretentious—a desk and a chair—plain, sturdy brown-stained furniture, as rugged as the Canadian timber from which it was hewn. Fred rapped on the desk with his knuckles. It had a solid, satisfying sound. Yes, it would do fine, he thought, and it would be good to have it around to remind him of his parents with their simple, practical wisdom and rustic honesty. The desk and chair were destined to serve him for the rest of his life, going with him wherever he moved.

A few days later, he marched out to the lawn with some tools and hung up a wooden sign that read:

DR. F. G. BANTING

On the front door he screwed a small brass plate containing the same simple inscription. Then he went back into his newly furnished office to wait for patients. None came. As the clock ticked away the seconds and then the hours, he began to feel uneasy. To pass the time he began to read, going painstakingly through his old medical books. The days went by and he continued his reading. Still no patients came. In fact, no one in the neighborhood gave the slightest hint of being aware that a new doctor had moved in.

Banting had hoped to become known as an orthopedic

specialist, to have other physicians refer cases to him, but this hope was soon dashed. It began to dawn on him that medical specialization was a new concept in London; that most general practictioners did not make referrals except in very special cases. And in such instances, they invariably sent their patients to the leading specialists in Toronto, such as Dr. Starr.

Soon he grew desperate. He longed to see any patient, orthopedic case or not, just as long as it was someone in need of medical help.

It was a full twenty-eight days before the first patient showed up! He was a laborer with a simple shoulder sprain, but Banting examined the shoulder and bandaged it as if he were performing major surgery.

At the end of his first month in practice, Banting's books showed a gross income of four dollars! Now he was faced with a critical decision. Doctors, too, must eat, and at this rate practicing medicine was a luxury he could ill afford. He applied for an instructorship at the University of Western Ontario. It was a part-time job teaching anatomy, physiology and clinical surgery. The salary was small, but at least it would help him get by until his practice caught on.

Almost immediately, Banting became popular with the students. They respected his quiet, authoritative manner in the classroom. When a question was asked, he gave a clear, honest answer. And when he didn't know the answer, he said so. Most important of all, he prepared his lecture material thoroughly, keeping up with the latest findings. Often, he would sit up half the night outlining the next day's work.

The students were also awed by his skill in the laboratory. Dissections were performed in a side room off the anatomy lab. His swift and sure way with a scalpel kept his classes alert and attentive, and during these demonstrations he kept up a lively commentary that amused as well as informed.

Although Banting enjoyed teaching, he enjoyed the laboratory work even more. Soon, he found that his old undergraduate interest in research had been reawakened, and he began to look around for a project to tackle.

The chief of the physiology department was Dr. F. R. Miller, a distinguished neurophysiologist. Before long, he asked Banting to join him in research work on how the outer layer of the brain, known as the cortex, reacts to external stimulation. The newly appointed instructor was delighted at the opportunity and accepted with almost indecent haste. Together, they performed a number of important experiments that proved Dr. Miller had been right when he asserted that the cortex is sensitive to outside stimulation, a theory that many medical experts had denied.

But these findings merely whetted Banting's appetite for research work. And since his private practice was still resoundingly unsuccessful, he found time to delve deeply into the latest research literature.

Soon he became the most frequent visitor to the university's medical library. Knowing of his interest in the latest medical findings, Miss Sullivan, the librarian, began to mark interesting reports in the new issues of the professional journals which she then put aside for her best "customer."

Banting's experience with blood transfusions in Toronto had stimulated his interest in this new medical technique. One day he discovered that a Dr. Ramsay of the medical school faculty was doing work in this field. He arranged to meet the researcher, and soon they were collaborating on experiments. Together, they performed the first successful

blood transfusion ever done in the London area. Their patient, a young child with anemia, was soon restored to health, and for the first time in his life Banting knew the wonderfully satisfying feeling that comes with doing research that has a direct application to bettering the lot of mankind.

But still Banting was not satisfied. He wanted more than anything else to do research, but research on a problem that he himself had carved out. When he wasn't teaching or reading in the library or working on the experiments of others, he paced restlessly in his tiny office on Adelaide Street North, waiting for patients who never came and dreaming bold dreams of making an important contribution to medicine.

In the evening he went out to dinner in a small, inexpensive restaurant, feeling frustrated at his failure to succeed in private practice and dissatisfied that he couldn't find a project into which he could wholeheartedly throw his energies.

He did have a few private patients, but these barely paid for his office expenses. His medical friends told him frankly that he was too devastatingly honest.

"You should adopt a more businesslike attitude," they warned him. "Your fees are much too low. Develop a bedside manner. People are impressed when you use complicated medical words. Then they go out and tell their relatives and friends. That's how to build up a successful practice."

But Banting would have none of it. "Maybe it *would* get me more patients," he replied. "But it wouldn't make me a better doctor."

One evening a member of the medical school faculty took

him to a meeting of the Shakespeare Club, a cultural society, and there he met Mary Healy, a professional artist. When she learned that as a child he had shown an aptitude for drawing and painting she encouraged him to try again. "Do take it up once more," she urged. "It's a wonderful way to relax."

Soon afterward, he was strolling along Dundas Street and paused in front of an art supply shop. Idly, he examined the window display of brushes, paints and other artist's materials. Then he resumed his walk, but about a block away he paused and returned to the shop. Perhaps Miss Healy was right. He *was* tense and bored. Why not try painting?

He purchased a portable easel, some colors and brushes. At home he unwrapped the package and began to mix paints cautiously. He dabbed at the canvas, gingerly at first, then more boldly. Finally he stepped back to examine his handiwork. It was a simple outdoor scene from memory. Not good, but not bad either, he told himself. It was years since he had painted, yet he found it satisfying. And perhaps he would be more successful as an amateur painter than as a medical practitioner. He returned to the easel, and it was two o'clock in the morning before he packed up his paints and went to bed.

During the following months he devoted all his spare time to his new hobby. On week ends he visited the park searching for scenes to sketch and paint. When he discovered an appealing landscape he set up his easel and went to work while children crowded around to watch him. He preferred to paint outdoor scenes, a carry-over from his boyhood fascination for the sloping hills and green fields of his father's farm.

Fred had a bold hand and a keen eye for colors. Soon he felt satisfied that he was making progress. But his brush technique needed improvement, so he secured a print of a fishing village scene by a famous artist and spent many days copying and recopying it. He painted the picture more than two dozen times before he felt convinced he was improving. It was the old laborious learning technique he had discovered in his early school years. It had brought him through medical school and through his residency. It was the only method he knew when he wanted to learn something new, this dogged technique of determination and hard work. It was tiresome and tedious but it brought results.

Painting succeeded in taking his mind off his problems and filled the long, empty hours of waiting for patients. By the time the summer of 1920 was over and autumn arrived, Banting no longer felt moody and discouraged. He was in a good frame of mind to welcome his new group of students.

He put his brushes aside to prepare his lecture schedule, poring through the textbooks and medical journals searching for classroom topics. Now here was an interesting subject: "The Pancreas, Ferment Factory of the Body."

He pencilled in the topic on his lecture schedule and jotted down October 31 as the date for the lecture. Then he made an additional notation in his pocket note pad to remind himself to dig up the latest material on the pancreas in the medical school library. He replaced the pad in his breast pocket and glanced up at the office clock, and was astonished to find it was almost nine. Suddenly he realized he was hungry as a bear, for he had not eaten a thing since noon.

• *CHAPTER FIVE* •

Hormone X

Nine out of ten medical school instructors would have considered Fred Banting an out-and-out fool. Here he was, a lowly lecturer on a part-time basis, receiving a pittance for pay; he had no tenure, few prospects for advancement. The lecture he was to deliver on the pancreas was purely a routine one. The vast majority of instructors, slated to deliver a routine talk to a class of second-year medical students, would have copied a few notes out of a standard textbook and let it go at that.

Not Banting. Night after night he waded through the latest research reports and medical journals, digging up new facts the textbooks didn't carry. According to his friends, it didn't make sense. And yet for Banting there was no other way. "If you're to do a job, boy, do it right," his father used to say. Thus, always deep within him was that nagging sense of duty, which had been drummed into him from childhood on.

That was why on those drafty October evenings of 1920 the young medical school instructor sat in his lonely office stuffing his head with obscure details about the small oblong gland behind the stomach that tears apart protein, starch and fat for the body to use.

Of course, as a physician Banting was well aware of the importance of the pancreas for digesting food. He knew, too, that it had something to do with the body's ability to use sugar. If the pancreas were removed, the blood and urine became charged with sugar, and the body died. There was nothing new in this fact. As far back as 1889, Von Mehring and Minkowski, two German researchers, had sliced out the pancreas of a dog, and within two weeks the unfortunate beast died of severe diabetes—or "sugar sickness" as it was sometimes called.

Diabetes! The dreaded word awakened unhappy memories in Banting. How many years had it been . . . fifteen? Yes, fifteen years had passed since he had marched in that pitiful little procession to the Alliston cemetery, carrying the casket of his friend Jane.

It had been a long time ago, and time is a great healer, for it puts sad memories to sleep, Banting thought. After so many years he could hardly recall what Jane looked like. She had golden hair and freckles—of that much he was certain. And she had been a pretty little girl, in spite of being a tomboy. But aside from that, her features eluded him now, hidden away in the dim recesses of forgetfulness.

Whether it was the rememberance of Jane or his own driving curiosity that now impelled him forward, Banting wasn't quite sure. But suddenly he felt an overpowering desire to find out more about this mysterious disease.

He began to study everything he could lay his hands on that dealt with diabetes. He searched avidly through his own medical books and haunted the medical school library. He checked through lengthy bibliographies and yellowed research reports. And in the end he was driven to the inescapable conclusion that although sugar sickness was as old as mankind itself, surprisingly little was known about it.

Egyptian hieroglyphics dating back four thousand years mentioned diabetes. And two thousand years after that, a Greek physician had given it its name. Astonishingly enough, the symptoms and development of the disease as described by these ancient medical writers coincided with those given by modern doctors in the latest scientific texts:

> The first warning sign is an enormous thirst and hunger that can't be satisfied. The urine and blood become overloaded with sugar. And soon the breath of the victim develops the penetrating odor of acetone, a chemical that is formed when body sugar is not digested properly. A feeling of tiredness and depression sets in. The patient grows frighteningly thin. In the final stages, he falls into a coma from which he never awakens.

Although these facts had been known for centuries, yet almost no progress had been made in treatment. Many distinguished doctors claimed diabetes was incurable and pessimistically predicted no advances would ever be achieved. In desperation, some physicians forced their patients to adhere to special diets to ward off the horrible final stages of diabetes as long as possible. But even when the diet worked for a time in such cases, it amounted to little more than slow starvation.

These, then, were the spotty facts Banting was able to uncover in his reading. But wait . . . there was one thing more. It had to do with the mysterious cells in the pancreas known as the islands of Langerhans. Now he recalled Professor McCallum's lecture in his own student days, when he had first heard mention of these baffling "islands." What was it McCallum had said? Although no one knew much about the Langerhans cells, they were reputed to contain a "secret treasure," he had declared. Banting smiled as he recalled the professor's colorful way of dramatizing ideas. A fine lecturer, McCallum, a master in the art of making complicated ideas sound simple, he told himself.

Now he went about the task of finding out all he could about the islands of Langerhans.

The pancreas is the body's ferment factory. It is connected to the small intestine by a duct. Through this duct, the pancreas pours forth a powerful digestive juice so food can be broken down in the intestine and used for the body's needs. In 1869 a sharp-eyed young medical student named Langerhans was peering through his microscope one day at a piece of pancreas and was astonished to find little bunches of spots. They looked like tiny islands. This strange group of cells was altogether different from the regular pancreas cells that produce digestive juice, for it did not lead to the intestine. In other words, the islands of Langerhans were found to be *ductless*.

The question scientists then began to ask themselves was this: If the Langerhans cells do not connect with the small intestine, what on earth are they used for? For a long time no one seemed to know the answer.

Finally, one curious researcher probed into the pancreas of patients who had died of diabetes. He was astounded to note that in such cases the islands of Langerhans looked sickly and shriveled, although the rest of the pancreas looked healthy.

At this point some physicians began to ask themselves whether these ductless cells had anything to do with diabetes. To prove that it was the islands of Langerhans rather than the rest of the pancreas that was associated with diabetes, one experimenter even chloroformed dogs and tied off the pancreatic ducts so not a drop of digestive juice could get out. When the dogs failed to get diabetes he felt he had proved his point.

As a result, a few scientists theorized that the Langerhans cells which are not connected to other body organs by ducts produce an unknown substance—Hormone X they sometimes called it—that is absorbed by the body in a mysterious way and helps it burn sugar for energy, thus preventing diabetes. But they had no idea of the exact nature of the hormone. Nor did they know how to obtain it.

Several daring researchers even tried feeding pieces of fresh pancreas to diabetic animals by mouth, but it did no good. Then they chopped it up and made extracts which they injected under the skin, but it, too, failed to halt the course of the dread disease. Even those who believed strongly in the theory became discouraged.

Of course, many medical authorities denied that such a thing as Hormone X existed. Others maintained that if this mysterious elixir *was* present in the body, there was certainly no proof of it. One of these experts was Dr. J. J. R. Macleod, head of the physiology department at the University of Toronto Medical School, Banting's old alma mater. He felt the Langerhans cells were nothing more than a "detoxifying center" which helped the body counteract poisons liberated during digestion.

So here was a tragic picture indeed. In all the nations of the world millions of people were sick with diabetes, thousands of them dying each week. And the sickest of all were innocent children who were struck down by it suddenly and without warning. In a short time the sugar sickness wasted them away to pitiful little skeletons, and invariably the younger victims died. But regardless of age, the symptoms were always the same—ravenous hunger and thirst. And the more the patient ate and drank, the more the sugar charged into his blood and urine until eventually he fell into a dreadful coma from which the only way out was death.

The facts depressed Banting. Was there no hope at all? It surely seemed that way. After all, for nearly a century the best medical brains in the Western Hemisphere and abroad had wrestled with the problem. Yet they had come up with no more than a few isolated facts, all of which led to a blank wall beyond which no one seemed able to penetrate.

It was the afternoon of October 30, 1920. Banting was to give his pancreas lecture the next day. It had taken a lot of time—much more time than he had originally thought—to prepare his talk. What's more, he felt a vague sense of futility. Here he had labored to bring forth a mountain of factual information and had come up with nothing but a mouse.

Before leaving the medical school for the day, he stopped off at the library to return some material. As always, Miss Sullivan greeted him with a friendly smile. She reached into her desk and pulled out a copy of a medical journal, the November issue of *Surgery, Gynecology and Obstetrics.* "It's the latest issue," she said. "Just came in this morning. I thought you'd like to see it so I put it aside."

Banting thanked her, sat down at a reading table and thumbed through it idly. What was this? A twelve-page article with the highly technical title, "The Relation of the

Islets of Langerhans to Diabetes, with Special Reference to Cases of Pancreatic Lithiasis." The report was signed by a Dr. Moses Barron of Minneapolis.

Now here was a curious coincidence, Banting thought. For the past few nights he had done little but think about the Langerhans cells and diabetes; and here was an article on the same subject. Perhaps there was something in it he could use for tomorrow's lecture.

He asked Miss Sullivan if he could borrow the journal overnight, and that evening, Banting returned to his drab little office after dinner and began to read. It was a lengthy article, but as always he went through it carefully, rereading the difficult paragraphs until he was certain he understood them. Suddenly a particular section caught his eye. He turned back the page and reviewed it, then reread it a third time. Mentally, he translated the technical terms into simple language and found that the concept was quite simple. What Barron was saying was that in certain cases of gallstones, the stones block off the pancreatic duct. Then, when the patient dies and the pancreas is examined during the autopsy, it is found that the cells which produce the digestive juice for the small intestine have become shriveled up due to the blocking of the duct. *Yet the islands of Langerhans have remained perfectly healthy—and such people did not have the faintest symptom of diabetes.*

Dr. Barron's article pointed out that the same thing had been found true of dogs. Researchers had put them to sleep, cut them open and tied up the pancreatic ducts. Then a few weeks later the dogs were opened up again and the pancreases examined. It was found that while the digestive juice cells had deteriorated because of the tied-up ducts, the Langerhans cells remained healthy, just as in the case of human gallstone victims. And like the gallstone cases, there was not a sign of diabetes in the dogs.

As the impact of Barron's article hit him, Banting tingled with excitement. By George, he thought, this is important! How did it fit in with the previous material he had gathered for his lecture? He fumbled through the notes he had written and mentally organized his findings.

First, Von Mehring and Minkowski cut out the entire pancreas of a dog, and the animal comes down with diabetes. This means that diabetes is associated with the pancreas.

Then, researchers probe the pancreas of dead diabetes victims and find the Langerhans cells sick and shriveled.

Finally, along comes Barron to say that gallstone victims or dogs with blocked or tied-off pancreases suffer from a shriveling of the regular pancreas cells. But the islands of Langerhans remain healthy and do not develop diabetes.

This would seem to prove that the Langerhans cells are associated with diabetes, probably through the production of an unknown hormone that helps the body burn sugar.

All right. But if this were so, why can't diabetes be controlled by feeding the victim pieces of healthy pancreas or injecting healthy pancreas extract under the skin? It sounded logical enough, and yet every time it had been tried, the technique failed. Why?

Banting's head was buzzing now. Barron's article had given him the germ of an idea. Now a spark caught his imagination and his brain took fire.

The pancreas produces a powerful digestive juice, he reasoned. Experimenters in the past had used minced pancreas or extract made of the *whole* gland. Was it possible that the strong digestive fluid destroyed the hypothetical hormone produced by the Langerhans cells while the pancreas was being chopped up or extracted?

But Barron's article said that by tying off the pancreatic ducts researchers had managed to kill the cells producing the powerful digestive ferment while keeping the Langerhans islets alive and healthy. Now what if an extract were to be made from such a gland? Wouldn't it then give a diabetic the full benefit of Hormone X without interference from the strong digestive juice?

It was a bold theory, Banting admitted to himself, and unproved. But isn't every theory unproved until it has been tried?

Excited by the sheer daring of the idea, he stared at the pages of Barron's article before him, no longer seeing the print. He wanted to talk with someone about his theory—anyone. He wanted to shout it from the rooftops. And what's more, he wanted to do it tonight. It couldn't wait, for if he went to bed without first getting it out of his system he wouldn't get a wink of sleep.

He thought of Dr. Tew, who had talked him into going to London in the first place. Tew had been practicing in London since August, and they had seen a good deal of each other. He would go over to see Tew right now and tell him all about it. Of course, it was nine o'clock in the evening, a bit late to go visiting. But this was too big, too important to keep to himself, even for a minute. He started to put on his overcoat, then remembered. The car . . . he had left it in the garage to be repaired.

He telephoned Tew. "Hello," he said with suppressed excitement. "This is Fred. If you're not doing anything, could you come over? I have something to show you."

Dr. Tew drove over within half an hour. Banting told

him everything and showed him the Barron article. Tew scratched his chin thoughtfully.

"I know how to set a broken leg or write out a prescription," he said. "But research and theory has never been my game. I must confess that most of this is lost on me. However, from what you've told me, Fred, I think you've hit on something. Why don't you talk to Professor Miller at the medical school, the one you did the cortex stimuli work with. Maybe he'd be willing to work with you on this."

Tew left shortly after midnight. For the next two hours, Banting paced restlessly back and forth in his tiny bedroom, chain-smoking cigarettes. Finally, at two o'clock in the morning he took out his little pocket notebook and wrote the following words: "Tie off pancreas ducts of dogs. Wait six or eight weeks. Remove and extract."

It was a simple notation, but one that was destined to make medical history.

The next day Banting delivered his lecture on the pancreas, the one that had started him off in the first place. It was well received by the students. But by this time the talk itself was of secondary importance. Banting had bigger things on his mind.

Later in the afternoon he caught Professor Miller in his office. He explained his whole theory. The older man admitted it sounded logical enough but explained that he couldn't help.

"My field is the physiology of the nervous system," he declared. "The project you've outlined is in endocrinology. I'm afraid it's way out of my line, Banting."

Miller added, too, that he was about to undertake further experimental work on the brain and would have time for nothing else in the near future. In fact, he had hoped that

Banting would continue to work with him on the new research, for he considered him a first-rate research assistant. But now that he had a laboratory project of his own he wished him the best of luck. Professor Miller did suggest, however, that Banting go to the University of Toronto to see Professor J. J. R. Macleod, who was considered a leading authority on sugar chemistry in the body and a spokesman against the theory that the Langerhans cells produce a mysterious Hormone X that helps the body burn sugar.

Banting now approached other medical school officials for help. Each gave him the same advice: Go see Macleod. He went to the dean to ask for a research appointment to work on Hormone X but was turned down. Macleod is your man, the dean said flatly. He's the one to ask for help since he's the expert in the field.

Banting was deeply disappointed, but he sat down and wrote to Professor Macleod for an appointment.

On a cold, clear morning in November he climbed into his rattly Ford and barreled out of London toward Toronto. The brisk autumn weather didn't bother him, for he was heated to a fever pitch by his compelling belief in his scheme.

It had been five months since he had last seen Toronto. Now, as he drove through the familiar streets he got a feeling of nostalgia, not unlike the feeling he had while visiting Alliston after a long absence.

His first stop, of course, was at Mrs. O'Neil's. As always, she was delighted to see him and made him stay for lunch. She also insisted that he plan to sleep over. Banting protested that he wanted to return to London that night, but she cut him short.

"Nonsense," she said. "You've had a long drive and you

look weary already, though it's only past noon. You'll stay here tonight, my lad, make up your mind to it. There will be fresh linens in the spare bedroom, and I'm certain I don't have to tell you how to make yourself at home at the O'Neil's!"

At last he agreed. From past experience he knew that once Mrs. O'Neil made up her mind, it was impossible to budge her.

In the afternoon he walked the short distance to the University of Toronto Medical School from which he had been graduated less than four years before. Professor Macleod was chairman of the Department of Physiology, and fifteen minutes before the scheduled time, Banting was already waiting outside the physiology offices, impatiently glancing at his watch.

Finally, an assistant ushered him in and showed him the chairman's private office. Macleod, a brisk little man, was sitting behind a huge desk. He asked Banting to take a seat.

"I am pleased to meet you, Dr. Banting," he said, his voice taking on a businesslike tone at once. "What can I do for you?"

The younger man began to fish for words. It would have to be exactly the right words to impress a man like Macleod. He felt his old shyness returning. He began to explain his theory, then got confused and started over again. Overanxious now, he desperately pulled out his little notebook and read the three sentences he had written down in those early morning hours of October 31. Then, realizing the words didn't say much by themselves, he tried a new tack: He began to review the past work done in diabetes research.

"Yes, yes," Macleod finally broke in impatiently. "Since

this happens to be my own special field, I'm quite aware of those findings. Please get to the point, Dr. Banting."

Fred ran his hands through his sandy hair. It was almost a gesture of nervous despair.

"What I'd like, sir, is a chance to show I can get a pure Langerhans extract by tying off the pancreatic duct and shriveling the digestive juice cells," he stammered. "Then I intend to prove this extract will keep diabetic animals alive —dogs, to be more exact."

There, he had said it. Now it was Professor Macleod's move.

Macleod stared at the young man for a long moment without saying anything. The expression on his face seemed to say: Who is this presumptuous neophyte with the longish, inquisitive-looking nose, and what are his qualifications for such a project?

Finally, he spoke: "I don't mean to sound condescending, Dr. Banting, but will you please outline your previous training and experience in research?"

Banting was stumped. He knew his answer would sound absurd, but he had no alternative. "None, really," he replied. "I worked for a short time with Dr. Miller at the University of Western Ontario on cerebellar cortex stimulation and with Dr. Ramsay there on blood transfusions. But frankly it was so limited that I guess it doesn't mean much."

Macleod told him that for many years, the world's leading researchers had tried to find a way to control diabetes. They had failed. They had also failed to isolate this hypothetical hormone that was alleged to exist—and he, for one, wasn't convinced that it did exist. Yet, in the face of these failures by scientists with many years of research experience, here was a young orthopedic surgeon with virtually no training or previous work in laboratory investigations who was convinced he could do what the others had failed to do.

No, Macleod declared, in all honesty he could not say he was impressed with Banting's plan. Certainly, in the face of his visitor's lack of background for the project, he, Macleod, could not take the responsibility of investing the medical school's funds and facilities in such a risky undertaking. He was terribly sorry but . . .

Banting left, feeling more disappointed than ever before in his life. On the way back to Mrs. O'Neil's he began to blame himself for his failure. If only he'd expressed himself more clearly . . . pleaded a little harder . . . if only . . .

That night at the dinner table he toyed with his food. Mrs. O'Neil, with her common-sense wisdom, sensed his mood immediately and did not say a thing. After dinner they sat in the parlor. While Mrs. O'Neil sewed silently, Banting stared morosely at the ceiling. Earlier, he had told her all about the interview with Macleod. While his former landlady did not have the foggiest notion of what "this queer business with the glands" was all about, she understood well enough how much it meant to him.

After a while, Catherine O'Neil put her sewing aside. "Now listen to me, lad," she said quietly but firmly. "Think me an interfering old Irish biddy if you will, but I've come to consider you like my own son. You know that, don't you?"

"I know that, Mrs. O'Neil," he replied dispiritedly.

"Well now, if you want my advice, I think it's wrong to hold any hard feelings against this important professor," she said. "After all, if he's as big a doctor as you say, he must have little enough time to waste. And there are some I know who would think it mighty nice that he gave you any of his time at all."

"I know that, too," Banting admitted.

"Now then, d'you think it would serve a purpose to go back to him tomorrow?" she continued. "Perhaps he'll have had a change of heart."

"Not a chance," he replied. "He was pretty definite when he turned me down. By now he probably doesn't even remember I'm alive."

"Look, Fred," Mrs. O'Neil persisted, "as I've already said, I'm just an ancient busybody and I know nothing about your medicines and those heavy doctor books you read. But I do know something about Fred Banting. You're not one of those slick young upstarts fresh out of school, with little more than a gift for the blarney to help them make their way. There's a shyness about you that keeps you from speaking your mind free and clear, but underneath you know more than nine out of ten of them. Now what if you were to scribble out what you wanted to say on a piece of paper and let this professor read it? Why, it would say the thing the way it should be said."

Banting stared at Mrs. O'Neil blankly for a moment. Then, as the impact of what she had said penetrated, he brightened. She was right, of course! A blockhead he'd been —why hadn't he thought of it? A statement outlining his proposal, a typewritten statement! That was the way busy administrators liked to have things done. They wanted everything set down in black and white. That way, too, he could express himself exactly as he wanted to, without stammering or beating around the bush. Besides, even if Macleod turned him down again for the time being, the statement would have the virtue of remaining on the professor's desk afterward. And who knows, after thinking about it for a while, he might reverse himself . . .

Banting felt like kissing Mrs. O'Neil in gratitude—and he did. Then he borrowed Anna O'Neil's battered old typewriter and sat down to work. He didn't finish until long after Mrs. O'Neil and the girls, who had spent the evening with friends, were asleep. But finally he had a neatly typed statement outlining his idea in simple, forceful terms but in sufficient detail to indicate he had spent a good deal of time thinking it out carefully.

He reread the statement for the last time, then folded it neatly and put it in his pocket. Yes, such an outline would appeal to an administrator's penchant for having things put in precise form.

Banting tiptoed up to the spare room, undressed and climbed into bed. He felt much more encouraged now, but he was still anxious and found it difficult to fall asleep. When finally he did, it was a fitful, restless sleep.

The next morning he was up early. After breakfast, he telephoned for another appointment and was pleasantly surprised when Macleod agreed to see him again without offering any resistance.

When he arrived at the medical school, he was shown into the office after only a few minutes' wait. The famous physiologist was again seated behind his huge old-fashioned desk. After some preliminary words, Banting handed him the statement.

Macleod read the paper carefully. It was well prepared, he told himself. Certainly it presented a stronger case than Dr. Banting had done yesterday. Moreover, he himself had given the matter additional thought and concluded that he had been too abrupt with this young man. Not that he felt the plan would succeed, for to any experienced researcher it seemed overly simple—almost harebrained in its simplicity. How in the world could a novice, with almost no research experience, hope to succeed where the best professionals had failed?

And yet he couldn't help thinking that the brightest pages in the history of mankind had been written by brash young amateurs who didn't have sense enough to admit defeat in advance . . .

Macleod laid the paper on his desk and stared out the window of his office. For a long while he didn't say a word. Then he turned to Banting. "I'm going to give you your chance," he said quietly. "What will you need for your experiments?"

The words hit Banting with the impact of a steam roller. He replied as one in a daze, almost without being aware of what he was saying. "I'll need the help of someone who knows biochemistry, a place to work for eight weeks, and ten dogs."

"I'll see that you shall have exactly that," Macleod declared briskly. "No more, no less. You'll have confirmation in writing within the week. Now, if you'll excuse me, I have to attend a faculty meeting."

Banting left, walking on air.

• *CHAPTER SIX* •

Exploring the Magic Islands

Banting wanted to plunge into the search for Hormone X immediately. He saw no reason for delay. The successful interview with Macleod merely fired his enthusiasm all the more. The idea burned in him like a fever that refuses to die down. And dreamer that he was, he wanted to give up everything at a moment's notice—his teaching, his ludicrous little practice, even the house he had just purchased—to follow his will-o'-the-wisp.

The more practical of his friends tried to talk him out of it. They didn't want him to burn all his bridges behind him. "At least finish out the year in London," they urged him. "That way, you'll have something to go back to." Even Dr. Starr, who did not feel Banting was on a fool's errand as did some of the others, made it clear he thought his protégé was getting soft in the head for wanting to give up his surgical career before he had barely gotten started.

But Banting refused to listen. There had always been a streak of stubbornness in him, and now it showed itself, sharp and clear. The more his friends argued against it, the more impatient he was to get his project underway. He quit his teaching post at the University of Western Ontario and no longer even pretended to be interested in building a practice.

Only his parents and Mrs. O'Neil, who understood him so well, did not try to talk him out of it. "There is no right or wrong in this matter," his father told him one week end while he was visiting the farm. "The right way is what you yourself think is right. It is Fred Banting—no one else—who will gain or lose. So it is Fred Banting who must decide."

Mrs. O'Neil, whom he had waltzed around the parlor after the successful second talk with Macleod, said much the same thing. Then she added, "After all, a body's never in the wrong when he's in a hurry to do good for humanity."

But in the end there *was* a delay, and it was Professor Macleod who insisted on it. When Banting pleaded that he wanted to get started at once, the chairman wrote back that because the school year had already begun, a delay until spring would give Banting more time to work out the details of the experiment.

The news was like an unexpected blow on the head. Here it was November, and he was being told he would have to wait at least six months. After the initial shock wore off, anger took its place. He was furious at administrators—all administrators. Chainsmoking angrily in his little office, he raved against regulations, red tape and all the other manifestations of officialdom.

A little later, he sheepishly realized that his attitude had been childish, but he also recognized that it had served a useful purpose, for it had given him a chance to blow off steam. He was convinced that if he had not permitted himself the luxury of such an outburst he very likely would have exploded.

As it turned out, Macleod was right. The delay could be

put to good use, Banting discovered. He began to haunt the library again in order to add to his earlier knowledge of diabetes and the pancreas. He also did a good deal of planning in terms of the surgical procedures he would have to use. Before long, he could recite the details in his sleep.

When he wasn't thinking or reading about diabetes, he painted or devoted his time to the outpatient department at Victoria Hospital in London. He worked on the orthopedic cases. One of his patients was a little boy of five who was missing one foot. The tiny youngster was very self-conscious about his deformity and always kept it hidden behind the good leg as he sat in his little wheel chair.

Banting was faced with a deep problem of applied psychology as well as orthopedic medicine. But he managed to solve it. He made a plaster cast of the good leg and then, at his own expense, took it to a shoemaker. He explained to the cobbler by means of a diagram that he wanted a laced cuff made of strong leather. Then he asked the hospital workshop to make up a small wooden foot. With these items and a pair of light, strong side braces of steel, he constructed an artificial leg. The father of the little boy brought the unused shoe and it was placed on the brace. Then Banting laced it to the child's leg. It resembled a natural foot so closely that the youngster was delighted. Later, Banting wrote of the experience:

> I shall always remember the look on the boy's face when he stood up in his new outfit. He walked—then he ran—then he jumped on it and could not take his eyes off it. Instead of tucking it under the chair, he put it out for everyone to see. The whole thing only cost me a few dollars and I was more pleased than the boy.

Some years afterward, Sir Robert Jones, acknowledged as the world's greatest living British orthopedic surgeon, visited London. While there, he examined the splint and termed it a "masterpiece."

But in spite of his attempts to fill the long winter days with useful work, the weeks and months seemed to drag by for Banting. By the time the trees and shrubbery blossomed in their green spring finery, he was almost counting the hours until he could go to Toronto.

Finally, May arrived. On a sun-kissed morning with the smell of freshly mowed grass in the air, he piled a trunk and two suitcases in the back of the car and bade good-by to London.

When he arrived in Toronto, he found that Macleod had kept his promise—to the letter. There were to be ten dogs at his disposal and a bench in a small chemistry laboratory on the second floor of the medical school building. He himself was to hold no official title and would receive no salary.

Banting was frank to admit his lack of familiarity with the latest biochemical techniques. Macleod solved the problem by making an announcement to the graduating class in physiology and biochemistry. He informed them that a young surgeon from London, Ontario, was going to do some experimental work on the pancreas during the summer and suggested that if any student were interested in taking part in this research, an opening was available. "Of course," he told them, "the experiments may not turn out to be very successful. But it would be very good experience for anyone who is seriously interested in medical research."

Two of the most brilliant members of the class responded. Both had spent the past term in experimental studies of diabetes and knew something about sugar metabolism.

Their names were Charles H. Best and E. C. Noble. Macleod told Banting that either one would make a first-rate assistant.

In the end, Best got the job. Noble was not very strong, and when his parents urged him to spend his vacation at home where he could rest up, he gave in. Best lived a good distance from Toronto and had previously made up his mind to spend the summer in the city so he could earn money for his next year's tuition at medical school. After listening to Banting's theory, however, he was so enthusiastic that he decided to forget about a salaried job.

Best was eager to work on Hormone X for another reason, too—a very personal reason. Just a few years before, his favorite aunt, Anna, who had been working as a nurse in Boston, had developed severe diabetes and died from it.

They were a curious team, Banting and Best. Physically, they were as different as night and day. At twenty-nine, Banting was spare, tense and muscular, with the rugged features of a farmer. Best, on the other hand, was only twenty-one, tall, fair haired, well scrubbed and athletic looking.

But they were brothers under the skin. Both had the peculiar stubbornness and dedication to a cause that is the mark of the scientific researcher. They were both idealists, willing to sacrifice personal needs and comforts to pursue a half-baked dream they believed in.

Once the spirit of the search caught him, Best's enthusiasm matched Banting's. His previous work on diabetes had given him experience and skill in using chemical methods to measure exact amounts of sugar in the blood and urine. Because of his intensive training in the four-year course in physiology and biochemistry, he was accurately informed on the latest techniques, many of which were unfamiliar to Banting.

Actually, Banting had expected that Macleod would assume final responsibility for the experiments. He had hoped to get valuable guidance from him. Then he learned that Macleod was planning to vacation in Scotland for the entire summer, and he and Best would be entirely on their own. Although it was another minor disappointment, it failed to shake his confidence, either in his idea or in himself.

On May 16, 1921, the two unpaid researchers stood alone in their little laboratory and tried to decide how to begin. It had all seemed so simple on paper, this business of exploring the magic islands of Langerhans. But now that they were about to begin, a tense excitement seized them.

Banting, puffing on a cigarette, stared silently at Best, and Best stared back at Banting. It was a warm spring day. Through the open door of the laboratory they could hear the barking of the dogs in their cages two floors above.

"Well, where do we start?" Best asked quietly.

Banting paused, then crushed out his cigarette. "We start at the beginning," he said, suddenly and decisively.

So they began at the beginning. During the following days they spent most of the time working in the hothouse of an attic where they operated on their dogs. With the sweat pouring down his face, Banting's scalpel slash-slashed with lightning speed as he cut open the stomachs of anesthetized animals. Then he reached in with his clever surgeon's fingers and deftly tied off the pancreatic ducts, using catgut. Finally, he sutured the wounds, and Best carried the unconscious dogs back to their cages.

Since it was their first try, they had operated on only a

few of the animals. But within a week it was obvious that all were recovering beautifully. The two researchers grinned at each other reassuringly.

Step two was not quite so simple. An elementary duct-tying operation was one thing. But removing the entire pancreas as the German researchers Von Mehring and Minkowski had done many years before, was something else again. Banting and Best soon discovered that inducing a state of diabetes in this manner, without killing the animal, was an involved and difficult task.

At first, Banting tried a surgical technique devised by a Frenchman named Hédon, in which the pancreas is removed in two stages. But this called for first-rate operating facilities which they didn't have. The result was a minor tragedy. Their first canine patients died of shock and infection.

Desperate, Banting set out to improvise a different method. Now, for the first time, he was grateful for his training as a surgeon. Until now, he had been led to believe by everyone—and, indeed, had come to believe it himself—that surgical experience is hardly a preparation for research work. In fact there had been times when he would have traded his entire four-year career as a surgeon for a solid year's experience in a laboratory.

But at this particular moment, the picture changed. Here was a problem for a surgeon and his past experience would be a help rather than a hindrance. How many times in the smoke of battle had he been called upon to devise emergency operating procedures to keep a soldier alive? Well, here was just such an emergency.

What Banting did was to perfect a technique of removing the entire pancreas in a single operation. It called for bold, delicate surgery and split-second timing. But it worked. By thus performing the pancreatectomy in a single stage, the chance of shock and infection was reduced. Even Best, who had admired Banting, the researcher, gained a new respect for the steel-nerved surgeon with the marvelously skilled fingers.

Now that they had licked the problem of removing the pancreas and giving a dog diabetes, they sat back to wait. They would wait for the digestive juice cells to degenerate in the animals with the tied-off ducts. Then they would see if Hormone X actually did exist . . .

In his little pocket notebook on that wild night in October, Banting had written: "Tie off pancreas ducts of dogs. Wait six or eight weeks . . ." The waiting was the difficult part. All during the hot June nights they waited, tending their dogs, even training them for their own amusement.

Before long the dogs became their pets. Their concern for the welfare of these animals was deep and genuine. Each dog was given a number, in most cases meaningless numbers. Sometimes the number was a date, occasionally the designation of a cage. In a few instances, Banting felt that a particular number suited a particular dog's personality. There was Dog 92, a yellow mongrel whom Banting referred to as a "collie hound" because he looked like "Collie," his own childhood pet, long since dead. There was Dog 409, a frisky Irish terrier who became one of their favorites. And there was Dog 55, a big, clumsy white bull mongrel who developed a special affection for Best.

Banting held to a deep conviction that the dogs were soldiers in the war against disease and therefore deserved only the finest treatment. He likened them to patients in a military hospital and insisted that they be given only the best food, plenty of water and kept in spotlessly clean cages.

Soon, the dogs were allowed the privilege of running about the laboratory freely, except when specimens of urine were required. Banting and Best even trained them to give blood willingly. When a blood sample was needed, Banting whistled, and the dog leaped upon the laboratory table and allowed itself to be laid on its side. Then it stuck out its paw. A towel was placed over the head and the vein in the leg was distended by an elastic band. When the blood had been taken, the towel was removed, and the dog jumped up to receive its reward—a piece of meat. Afterward, it romped gaily around the room until the next blood sample was needed.

Banting devised a technique for obtaining blood painlessly and without injuring the dog's health. In most laboratories, samples were taken by anesthetizing the animal, slashing the skin and exposing a large vein. Afterward, the vein was tied off and the skin sewed up. But after a few samples were obtained, the vein would be used up. Moreover, repeated doses of anesthetic endangered the dog's health.

Banting considered this method cruel. He experimented until he found that with care he could insert a fine needle into the vein directly through the skin, as with a human. Then, by using the same hole in the skin each time, he could secure repeated samples without pain or danger to the dog.

As the weeks went by, the two unpaid experimenters began to feel the pinch of poverty. The cash Banting had scraped together to support himself during his flyer in scien· tific research was fast dwindling. Best also needed money.

His father, a physician, could have helped him, but the youth refused to ask for it. This was a personal challenge he was determined to meet on his own.

During the stifling summer nights, they sat in the laboratory, cooking meals over a Bunsen burner, smoking and talking. They talked about a lot of things—the unbearable heat, politics, the future of medical science. But most of all they spoke of diabetes, of the millions of diabetics in all the countries of the world and what it would mean to these doomed sufferers if it turned out that Banting's hunch about Hormone X was right. They even invented a name for the hypothetical hormone.

"We'll call it isletin," Banting said, "because it comes from the islets of Langerhans. What do you say?" Best agreed. To an outsider it might have seemed ludicrous to hear these two amateur researchers, who didn't have enough cash in their pockets for a square meal, talking about revolutionizing the world of medicine.

July sixth! It was now seven weeks since Banting had tied off the pancreatic ducts of the first batch of dogs. Originally, he had estimated six to eight weeks as the time needed for the digestive juice cells to shrivel. Now he decided the time had come to reoperate. He would split the time difference.

Up the stairs they climbed from the little chemistry laboratory to the dog room in the attic. The smell of chloroform was strong as Best put two of the dogs to sleep. Banting's gleaming scalpel flashed as he made the incisions and he peered eagerly through his thin-rimmed spectacles at the oblong pancreas. Both he and Best knew that the cells should be dead by now, leaving only pure, healthy islands of Langerhans—the source of the magic hormone.

But what was this? Something had gone terribly wrong. In these two animals the pancreas had *not* degenerated at all. In these two dogs it was still full sized and perfectly healthy!

Banting muttered angrily under his breath and called Best over to confirm his own observation. It was true. "But what could have caused it?" he asked.

"I don't know," Banting told him. "But I'm going to find out." With his scalpel he gently cut around the ducts he had tied off so carefully. "Now this is odd," he murmured to Best. "The catgut is coated with pus. What do you suppose that means?"

Suddenly it hit him. Of course—he had committed a stupid, schoolboy blunder! In his anxiety to cut off every last drop of digestive juice from flowing through the ducts, he had tied them off too tightly. As a result, gangrene had set in under the catgut, and a new duct had grown around the surface of the old one. It was Nature's way of compensating for the infection.

Now they were in a real dilemma. There was only a week left in the eight weeks allotted by Macleod, and they were no further along than when they started!

It was a serious setback, Banting admitted to Best, but he wasn't going to give up yet. He asked Best to bring the other duct-tied dogs to the operating table. In a frenzy of activity he opened their stomachs and examined each pancreas in turn.

"Look," he shouted to Best. "We haven't failed altogether." In a few of the animals, he had apparently tied the catgut just right, and the pancreases were degenerating nicely.

Now Banting retraced the first step and performed the

duct-tying all over again. But this time he knew what to avoid. He would have to work more delicately, as if he were walking a tightrope. He conjectured aloud, "If the catgut isn't tight enough, the digestive juice will flow." Best nodded. "If it's too tight, gangrene will set in. Now lets see, what's the best compromise?"

He solved the problem by tying each duct in two or three places. Each ligature was tied with a different degree of tension. His reasoning was superbly simple: If one ligature proved to be too tight, the second would do the job. And if *it* didn't work, the third would.

In the case of the dogs whose pancreases had already degenerated, he allotted an additional two weeks. This way he would be absolutely certain to have nothing but pure Langerhans cells to work with.

Once again they waited. It was past the eight-week limit now. Each day they expected a letter from Professor Macleod in Scotland ordering them to stop the experiments. But no letter came. "Do you suppose he's decided to give us an extension?" Best asked. "Or maybe he's forgotten all about the project?" Whatever the reason, it was a reprieve, an unexpected gift, and Banting was grateful for the additional time.

Then a new crisis arose. The last of Banting's money had run out, and he was flat broke! For one thing, the original allotment of ten dogs was gone, so he had been spending his own money to buy more. He now realized how naïve he had been in his original request. Instead of ten dogs, he should have asked for twenty, thirty, even fifty.

But it was too late now. More dogs were needed—and more dogs they would have. Banting sold his Ford. With the money in his pocket he and Best went out into the streets of Toronto to search for dog owners. They knocked at doors and stopped people in the streets. Some animal owners looked at them as though they were out of their minds and turned away brusquely. But there were others who needed cash and were willing to sell their dogs for a price.

July twenty-seventh turned out to be a miserably hot day. In the steaming medical school attic a pitiful dog, thin and burning with diabetic thirst, lay on the operating table. A week before, Banting had removed its entire pancreas. Now the animal was rapidly approaching the final coma.

For many hours Best had been taking blood tests. His colorimeter calculations showed the dog's blood choked with sugar. Thus the stage was set for the climactic moment. This was the dog and this was the time to test the theory.

On a second operating table near by, Best placed a duct-tied dog and administered chloroform. The two researchers were wearing lightweight white cotton operating gowns, but underneath the sweat poured out of their bodies and bathed them as if they had just stepped out of a shower.

Banting paused to take a deep breath and relax the tension that was gripping him. Finally he was ready. He stepped up to the dog and carefully, deliberately laid open the abdominal cavity. Then he displaced the stomach with the scalpel to reveal the shriveled leftover of what was once a pancreas. It had degenerated so that it was now barely the size of a human finger. But what was more important was the fact that the islands of Langerhans were still there, healthy and functioning.

After ligaturing, Banting calmly used his knife to sever the gland from its bed. He carefully removed it from the surrounding intestinal tissue and handed it to Best. The youthful researcher placed the pancreas in a chilled mortar which was standing in a solution of ice and salt water. He chopped it up into tiny pieces. The reason for maintaining it at low temperature was to prevent destruction of the gland in the summer heat and to keep it from being contaminated by bacteria. Now Best added Ringer's solution, a combination of various salts and water, and filtered the mixture through filter papers.

At last the moment had arrived! If Banting's theory were correct, the fluid Best had made should be an extract of Hormone X, more or less pure Hormone X, uncontaminated by the powerful pancreatic juice.

Best sucked the liquid into a syringe and handed it to Banting. The surgeon brushed the sweat from his eyes and bent over the neck of the dying diabetic dog. Gently and skillfully he inserted the syringe into the vein and pressed the plunger home. Then Best got to work drawing off the first blood sample. The animal lay on its side, its breathing slow and painfully labored . . .

They waited. For the next hour or so Banting and Best said little to each other. There was little they could say or do, except wait and see. Best busied himself with his colorimeter, testing the blood samples. Finally, after a long silence, he turned away from the instrument, almost in disbelief.

"Fred," he said quietly, "the blood sugar is down, down almost to normal."

But even without this information, Banting knew that a miracle was taking place. He had been keeping his eyes riveted on the dog. The animal, who had barely been able to stir a short time before, had now lifted its head and looked around the room. Finally, it raised its body from the table and sat up. A few minutes later its tail was wagging happily. And this was at a moment when, by all the known laws of medical science, it should have been dead!

For the next five hours they kept the dog under close observation. Its urine was sugar free by now, with less than one seventy-fifth the amount Best had measured on the previous day.

They had succeeded! By now there was no longer any doubt. They were rank amateurs, yet they had done what the world's leading researchers had failed to do in all their years of research. *They* had brought a diabetic dog back from the dead!

On that sweltering July evening of 1921, Fred Banting and Charles Best stood silently in the attic of the University of Toronto Medical School building and stared at the four-legged, tail-wagging miracle in front of them. They were too choked with emotion to realize how tired they were! For a long moment they had the curious and humble feeling of having touched the stars.

In years to come, medical historians were to describe the day's events as one of the most dramatic and brilliant chapters in the long and glorious saga of medical discovery.

• *CHAPTER SEVEN* •

The Treacherous Shoals

The next day the dog was dead.

Sometime during the early morning hours, while Banting and Best were catching a few winks of sleep, the diabetic canine hero suffered a relapse. Soon he fell into a coma. And by late morning he was beyond help.

Now they had learned something new. This magic soup of theirs did not *cure* diabetes. But it did stop it dead in its tracks on a temporary basis.

Yet somewhere deep within Banting was a nagging doubt. Not self-doubt as to the correctness of his theory, for of that he was instinctively certain, as certain as his name was Fred Banting.

What did bother him was whether he had proved his idea, proved it so a professional researcher like Macleod would be satisfied. When the time came for the accounting with the physiology chairman, he would have to present black-and-white evidence, evidence so strong it left no room for doubt. And right now all he had was the body of a single dead dog who had lived for half a day beyond his allotted span.

"Dr. Banting," he could almost hear Macleod saying, "are you sure it was the extract of degenerated pancreas that lowered the blood sugar? Or could it have been a temporary phenomenon that might have been achieved just as well by an extract of, say, liver or spleen?"

All right. If that was the kind of proof Macleod would look for, he would give it to him. He would finish the experiment, finish it all the way.

Now he sliced out the pancreas of a second dog and waited until the unslakable thirst and hunger set in. Then he and Best went to work on another of their duct-tied dogs and brewed their queer cocktail of degenerated pancreas. But in addition, they also made extracts of liver and spleen. Then they injected the liver extract into the dying animal. It did nothing at all for this poor animal who was almost too weak to keep breathing. They tried the spleen extract. But again nothing happened.

The laboratory-induced diabetes kept running its course unchecked. The dog was far gone. In a few hours he would be dead, there was no doubt of it.

In the dead of night, Banting once more shot a dose into the creature's vein, but this time it was the magic pancreas brew. Gradually, he increased the dose, injected another and still another. It worked like an eerie charm. The dog kept getting stronger by the minute. In a few hours, tests showed that his urine was free of every last drop of sugar. Hormone X worked, just as it had on the first diabetic dog.

Best used the degenerated pancreases from two other duct-tied dogs to make up additional quantities of extract. These were injected periodically. In this way they managed to keep their second miracle animal alive for three whole days.

They were elated. This was the kind of black-and-white proof Macleod could not dispute. They had shown beyond a shadow of a doubt that it was the pancreas extract and only the pancreas extract that kept the dogs alive.

But the elation was short lived. Suddenly a terrible truth dawned on them. Experimentally they had fashioned a miracle. They had found a laboratory stopgap for diabetes. However, to control sugar sickness they had to kill healthy animals. If this was the only solution—murdering the well to help the sick—then they had failed after all. The project was self-defeating, a dead end.

It was Marjorie, Dog 92, that dramatized the sheer horror of the dilemma. Marjorie—the "collie hound"—had become Banting's special favorite, his pet. She was a friendly, tail-wagging animal who was allowed to roam more freely than the rest about the laboratory and operating room.

Now she was a diabetic by virtue of having had her pancreas removed. For eight days they had kept her alive with their precious isletin. But it had taken the lives of five duct-tied dogs to do it. Finally there was no more extract left. Moreover, they had run out of duct-tied animals. It would take another eight weeks to shrink the pancreases of additional dogs.

Banting was beside himself with grief and hopelessness. Was there not a more practical way to get this mysterious stuff that helps the body burn sugar? It was a question he had been asking himself for days, but he was no closer to the answer. Now the situation was more desperate. Now the life of Marjorie, the dog that reminded him of his own childhood pet, was at stake. Hour by hour she was growing weaker. Soon, coma would set in . . .

Almost in a frenzy, Banting had Best make up a batch of extract from a fresh, whole pancreas, and he injected it into Marjorie. It was a forlorn hope. The injection had no effect at all, as they knew in advance.

Then another idea hit Banting. It was an experiment he remembered from his medical school days. A long, tedious experiment, but it was worth a try. It was a trick whereby the pancreas could be *overstimulated* to produce digestive juice until it wore itself out and could make no more. Once that happened, they could extract the pancreas without fear that the strong juice would injure the isletin.

So they put a healthy dog to sleep, one whose ducts had not been tied, and Banting made an incision. Best went to work drawing off liquid from the small intestine. It was the stomach's *secretin* he needed, a chemical that is produced in the intestine, enters the bloodstream and stimulates the pancreas.

For the next four hours, Banting injected the animal's secretin back into its own body while Best collected every drop of digestive juice manufactured in the hyperactive process. Finally, the gland exhausted itself and could produce no more.

Then Banting removed the entire pancreas. Best froze it, mashed it and made the extract. Then into the vein of Marjorie went the emergency ration. Even before Best's colorimeter could measure the blood sugar, strange things began to happen. Marjorie blinked her eyes and wagged her tail playfully. Within three hours she was romping happily around her cage. Banting opened the cage door and she leaped out, pleading to be scratched behind the ears. He was so overjoyed he could have cried.

But once more the success was short lived. They tried the exhausted pancreas technique again and again. They discovered it did not work every time. The business of wearing out the gland was a ticklish, delicate operation. And if it weren't done just right, the extract was not effective. Even so, they managed to keep Marjorie alive for twenty days.

It was now clear to Banting and Best that they had to come up with a practical method of obtaining large-scale quantities of isletin. And they couldn't do this by continuing to sacrifice healthy animals, either through tying the ducts or exhausting the pancreas itself.

While Banting thought hard about the problem, he and Best continued to operate on their dogs and refine their knowledge of isletin. In September, Macleod returned from Scotland. He checked their progress reports and asked to see a demonstration. The results were even more dramatic than before.

While conceding that the experiments looked promising, Macleod retained his customary caution. Still more evidence was needed, he insisted. He also informed Banting that since he would be busy doing work on other projects, they would have to continue their research alone.

Banting was not too happy at this lack of enthusiasm on the professor's part. But he told himself that at least Macleod was sufficiently impressed to permit them to continue using the medical school's facilities.

Now, in addition to the problem of producing large-scale supplies of isletin, money woes returned to plague them. The cash from the sale of the car was gone, and the two unsalaried researchers were at the end of their financial rope. Eating regularly had become a major problem.

Professor Velyien Henderson, chairman of the department of pharmacology, came to their rescue. Henderson had been impressed with Banting and his theory from the very beginning. Now he came forward with material help.

Henderson told Banting that a demonstrator in pharmacology had resigned, and the job was his if he wanted it. Banting accepted with the alacrity of a parched desert traveler who has just found an oasis.

The salary was small but at least it would enable them to buy food and other necessities. Theoretically, Banting was to teach pharmacology two days a week and be free to do his research the rest of the time. As it worked out, however, he did almost no teaching. But Henderson was satisfied with the arrangement, for in reality he considered the job a research appointment. To make certain there would be no later misunderstanding among the university officials, he went to Macleod and insisted that he write to the administration stating his belief that the isletin experiments would probably lead to something useful. Macleod haggled about the wording of the letter but finally agreed to Henderson's request.

Shortly afterward, Lady Luck smiled on Banting again. One evening he was reviewing medical literature on the pancreas and came across a paper Charlie Best had unearthed. It was by Laguesse, a Frenchman. In it, the researcher reported that he had found the pancreases of newborn human babies to be relatively richer in Langerhans cells than those of grownups.

This was interesting, Banting told himself, for if it were true of humans it must also be true of animals. He went to bed still turning the matter over in his mind. But it refused to let go, and he found himself unable to sleep.

Suddenly he sat upright as a fantastic scheme hit him. He bolted out of bed and spent the next hour pacing up and down, smoking and thinking. The hunch was very simple. If the islets of Langerhans were richly developed in newborns, they must be even richer in embryo animals before birth, he reasoned. Moreover, there would be no digestive juice present to poison the isletin. After all, digestion is not needed until after birth! Why hadn't he thought of it before?

The next morning he burst in on Professor Henderson. The pharmacology chairman listened intently as Banting outlined his plan. "The theory sounds fine," he observed wryly, "but I think you'll find that getting unborn puppies is something else again."

Banting winked slyly. "Not puppies," he said. "Calves. Embryo calves. It doesn't matter what animals we use to give us isletin. Were you raised on a farm?"

"No," Henderson admitted.

"Well, any good farmer knows that when he wants to fatten cattle for slaughter, the best thing to do is breed them first," Banting explained, "because pregnant cattle are better feeders. So the best place in the world to get embryo calves is in a slaughterhouse."

For the next few minutes, Professor Henderson listened with fascination as the former farm boy-turned-researcher lectured him on animal husbandry.

A little later, Banting picked up Best and they went out to a slaughterhouse some distance away. The foreman looked at them queerly when they explained what they had in mind. He was sure that they were two crazy scientists from the university, but probably harmless enough, so he gave them leave to poke around. By noon they were back in the laboratory with the pancreases of nine embryo calves.

Best mashed up the glands and made a good quantity of extract. It was marvelous the way it worked. Just as Banting had figured, it sent the blood sugar of their diabetic dogs spinning way down—down to normal.

Now they had solved another major worry. For the first time they were able to get plenty of isletin cheaply enough to step up the pace of the experiments. At this rate they would soon have enough trial results to satisfy even Macleod. But almost as important to Banting's peace of mind was the knowledge that they would no longer have to sacrifice the lives of healthy dogs just to obtain extract. When he compared their present affluence to the early days when every last drop of isletin was more precious than gold, he felt like a millionaire . . . At last, they were on their way to leaping the final hurdle—the problem of obtaining limitless supplies, enough to satisfy the needs of millions of diabetics throughout the world!

Of course the use of embryos was a giant step forward. It meant plenty of isletin for experimental purposes. But Banting was under no illusions that it was the final answer, for there simply weren't enough embryo calves available to provide daily doses for every human victim. And until the answer *was* forthcoming, he would have to keep searching —searching for a practical source that would place the magic fluid within the reach of every diabetic everywhere, the rich and the poor, the young and the old.

In the end, common sense gave Banting and Best their answer. They agreed that the only way to get more pancreas was from the slaughterhouses—pancreases from adult steers. The problem was how to cope with the digestive juice that contaminated the precious isletin. If only they could find a way to eliminate this powerful juice as a factor, their battle would be won.

It was painfully clear that tying off the pancreatic ducts

of the cattle before they were sent to be slaughtered was out of the question. So was the technique of injecting secretin to exhaust the glands. These were expensive, time-consuming processes that called for surgical skill. No, if they were to lick this problem it would have to be done by simpler means. The use of a chemical agent, perhaps, to *neutralize* the digestive fluid.

Actually, the approach was not entirely new. Ever since the first crude experiments back in July and August, they had tested various solutions in addition to salt water while producing the extract to see which would give the best results.

But now they went ahead in earnest. They began to use all sorts of solutions. It was a tedious and exhausting procedure, but by now they were accustomed to the laborious nature of research work. And the knowledge that they had come this far kept them going, even though the failures piled up.

Among the many different solutions they had tested were alcohol and acid in the hope that one or the other would effectively neutralize the pancreatic juice. But these had been used individually. Now Best remembered a chemical solution he had once used during a classroom experiment in his course at the university. "Why not use a combination of acid and alcohol," he suggested. Banting agreed it was a first-rate idea.

Best went to work. He took a whole beef pancreas and mashed it up in the usual way. Then he added the acid-alcohol mixture. Now he sucked it up into a syringe and handed it to Banting. A diabetic dog was already on the operating table waiting to be injected. Banting gently injected the needle into the animal's vein.

After a while, Best drew a blood sample and squinted into the colorimeter. The result was astonishing. "Fred," he said, "I think we've hit it this time. The blood sugar is testing out beautifully. It's way down."

The two experimenters were tense with excitement. At last they had succeeded in devising a method for producing unlimited quantities of isletin from the whole pancreas of newly slaughtered adult cattle, supplies sufficient to meet the needs of hundreds of thousands of diabetics throughout the entire world!

Now they were ready for the final step: testing isletin on human beings. Early in January Banting decided the time was ripe. He and Best made an extract from adult beef pancreases. Then they injected it into each other's arms. They waited. Aside from a slight reddening where the needle had been inserted, they felt no untoward effects.

These preliminary tests proved little, of course, except that isletin was not dangerous to human beings. But since neither Banting nor Best had diabetes, the important question still remained unanswered: would isletin control the sugar sickness in humans as it did in dogs?

On January 11, 1922, the first opportunity presented itself for the magic hormone to be used on a human diabetic. In Toronto General Hospital was a fourteen-year-old patient named Leonard Thompson. When he was admitted to the hospital he weighed less than sixty-five pounds. He was in the last stages of diabetes, and his case had been pronounced hopeless. The physicians shook their heads sadly and informed his parents that he would be dead in a matter of weeks, if not days.

When matters are hopeless, any slender straw is better than none at all. And this was true in the case of young

Leonard Thompson. The hospital officials told his parents there was little more they could do, but they asked permission to inject the lad with the new hormone prepared in a laboratory at the University of Toronto Medical School. They warned that the extract might not have any effect, but suggested that it was worth a try.

Leonard's parents had never heard of Frederick Banting or Charles Best. But they were desperate. They decided to leave the decision to the boy himself.

Leonard said yes.

A dose of isletin was injected. Almost immediately the blood sugar was reduced. But then the physicians noticed that a sterile abscess had formed at the site of the injection. The treatment was discontinued.

Banting and Best hurriedly prepared another batch of extract. At first a weak solution was used. Unlike the earlier batch, no harmful effects were observed. Gradually the doses were increased. The sugar that had been clogging the lad's blood began to disappear. The urine was tested and found to be sugar free. And with this remarkable change, the wretched symptoms of diabetes—the never-ending hunger and thirst—disappeared, too.

The isletin treatment was continued by the astonished hospital physicians. In a matter of days, Leonard Thompson was on his way to becoming as healthy as any other boy his age. The only difference was that from now on he would always have to take isletin to remain well.

Thus, less than nine months after they had started on their fantastic, epoch-making experiment, Dr. Frederick Banting and Charles Best had succeeded in restoring a diabetic child to health for the first time in the history of medicine!

• CHAPTER EIGHT •

INSULIN—Liquid That Saves Lives

At last Macleod was convinced. It had not been an easy task for he had insisted on solid proof. And in this matter he was absolutely correct. But Banting and Best had done it—had proved their case.

Macleod's amazement was all the greater when he realized that it had been done right under his very nose, without his being aware of the true significance of the experiments until the goal had been reached. It took him some time to adjust to the fact that the young orthopedic surgeon who had talked him out of ten dogs and the use of a laboratory, together with an unpaid assistant, had pulled off one of the greatest triumphs in medical history. For Banting and Best had done on a shoestring what the world's leading researchers had failed to accomplish with the finest and most up-to-date equipment.

Now, isletin was no longer a laboratory phenomenon. Its success with Leonard Thompson and other severe diabetics at Toronto General Hospital signified the dawn of a new day of hope for the victims of sugar sickness all over the world.

Once Macleod realized what was happening, he arrived at an important decision. He dropped his own work on anoxemia and turned over almost his entire laboratory staff to the task of purifying and refining Banting's extract. Among the researchers who joined the project were Dr. J. B. Collip, an expert in biochemistry, and E. C. Noble, who had been one of the candidates for the job of Banting's unpaid assistant the previous year.

Before long, Collip managed to devise a laboratory technique to get purified isletin by a complicated process known as "fractional alcoholic precipitation." This was an important step, because it showed that it was possible to eliminate impurities that might cause skin irritations and other harmful effects.

But when Collip's method was tried out on a large scale, all sorts of complications arose. Best was assigned to the task of ironing out the quirks, and he worked long hours in the university's Connaught Laboratories to get quantity production going as soon as possible. Before long, steady supplies were being made available for mass testing of human diabetics.

Macleod insisted that isletin's name be changed to "insulin." Actually, both names meant the same thing. They indicated that the hormone originated in the islets or islands of Langerhans. However, Macleod pointed out that insulin, which came from *insula,* the Latin word for islands, was easier to pronounce. Moreover, it had been suggested as far back as 1909 by various researchers as a good name for Hormone X should it ever be discovered. Banting agreed to the change of name.

One day he received a visit from an old friend, a physician and former army captain named Joseph Gilchrist. Gilchrist had graduated with Banting in "Meds Seventeen." Like Banting and the rest, he had gone into the Army right after graduation. A short time later, while in uniform, he had developed diabetes.

For five years, Joe Gilchrist had forced himself to adhere to a starvation diet to keep the dreaded sugar from choking his blood. He kept growing thinner despite the severe treatment he had imposed on himself. After his discharge from the Army in 1919, the diabetes continued to grow worse, and as a doctor he knew only too well the inevitability of his illness. He found it difficult to concentrate on his medical practice. He was morose a good deal of the time. Hunger gnawed at him constantly, and he was often too weak to drag himself on the rounds of his patients.

In October, 1921, while Banting and Best were desperately working on their scheme to produce life-giving insulin, Gilchrist suffered his worst blow. He came down with flu, an infection that was dreaded by every diabetic, for it tended to lower the body's sugar tolerance even more.

The next three months were sheer torture. He was starved, racked by thirst and so weak he could hardly stand up, yet he fought for life with an overwhelming tenacity. And just about this time he began to hear rumors, strange rumors about the work his old classmate Banting was doing with patients at Toronto General Hospital.

On February eleventh, a month after insulin had been injected into little Leonard Thompson, Joe Gilchrist showed up at the University of Toronto and asked to be directed to Dr. Fred Banting. He dragged his thin, tired body up the stairs to the second-floor laboratory, and there he offered himself as a human guinea pig.

Banting dreaded emotional outbursts, but he was so touched by Gilchrist's generous proposition that he had a hard time keeping from crying.

The first thing he did was to feed his old classmate thirty grams of pure glucose. Then Best administered a respiration test to see if the body was burning any sugar. This he did by having Gilchrist exhale into a wedge-shaped rubber container called a Douglas bag. The device enabled the researcher to measure the amount of carbon dioxide produced during breathing in relation to the oxygen absorbed. This ratio, known as the "respiratory quotient," indicated whether the body was utilizing sugar properly.

Even the routine task of breathing into the Douglas bag was a laborious chore for poor Gilchrist. Best checked the respiratory quotient, then double-checked it to make sure. He shook his head grimly. It was one of the severest cases of diabetes they had seen.

Banting now measured off a quantity of insulin in a syringe and jabbed the needle skillfully into Gilchrist's vein. There was nothing to do but sit around and wait, so they idled the time away by reminiscing about their medical school days.

An hour passed, then two. Best kept himself busy by taking regular respiration readings. But nothing happened. "It takes a few hours for insulin to really start working," Banting said reassuringly.

Gilchrist grinned weakly. "Don't worry, Fred," he said. "I'm not. After living with diabetes for a few years you don't have the strength to worry."

Banting had promised his parents he would be home for the week end. He didn't want to leave until there were clear cut test results, but Joe Gilchrist insisted that he go. "Don't worry, I'll be all right," he declared. Banting had barely enough time to make the train. He left instructions with Best to continue the sugar tests. A few minutes after he had gone, Charlie Best took another Douglas bag test.

It was amazing. The respiratory quotient had risen to 0.90, and a test of the urine proved it to be sugar free! Gilchrist himself could hardly believe it. "This is the first time it's been this way in five years," he told Best.

By this time his head felt clear. The weariness in his emaciated body had disappeared, and he felt as spry as a youngster. Although Best cautioned him to take things easy for a while, he hurried down the stairs two at a time.

When Gilchrist got home, the first thing he did was to telephone Banting's parents and ask them to pass on the good news when Fred got in. Then he sat down and ate a square meal. It was the first time he had eaten real food in so long he had almost forgotten what it tasted like.

From that day on, Dr. Joe Gilchrist was their "human rabbit." Each new batch of insulin was tested on him before being used on other patients. After a few months, Banting obtained permission from the Canadian government to use Toronto's Christie Street Hospital for Returned Soldiers to carry out further clinical tests, and he and Gilchrist became a testing team. Together they shot doses of insulin into the most severe diabetics, all of whom were veterans of the military services. Soon, health was flowing back into their emaciated bodies.

Some of those early tests were dangerous, particularly in cases where they had used overdosages. But Gilchrist always insisted that the experiments be tried on him first.

One day he injected himself with insulin. Suddenly he began to sweat, although the room was not warm. His legs began to buckle under and he felt himself about to collapse. He tried to think, but his brain refused to function. Frightened to a near-panic by now, some instinct forced Gilchrist to reach for a beaker of glucose. He raised it to his lips with trembling fingers and drained it down to the last drop. Soon, he felt himself returning to normal.

It was this incident and others like it that first served to warn Banting and Gilchrist and the others engaged in insulin research of the potential dangers of the new hormone if not used properly. It taught them that an overdose or even a normal dosage, when the body does not have sufficient sugar for the insulin to help burn up, can result in severe shock to the diabetic.

Another time Gilchrist suffered an "insulin shock" while strolling along the streets of Toronto. Dizziness cloaked his brain, and he began to weave unsteadily. A police officer arrested him, took him to the police station and booked him on charges of public intoxication.

When word reached the diabetic veterans at Christie Street, they were indignant. Immediately, they formed a delegation and rushed down to court to testify on behalf of "the Captain." The magistrate was extremely interested in what they had to say about insulin and asked a great many questions about the new miracle fluid. Finally, the "prisoner" was released with apologies from the court and the police.

The task of serving as a guinea pig during those early insulin tests was not pleasant. It was painful and full of discomfort. Minor toxic reactions such as swelling and redness were common. But Joe Gilchrist and some of the other veterans stuck it out. When Banting wrote about his classmate some years later he said, "There is probably not a person alive who has had more samples of blood taken from his veins."

Not all the early testing was done at Christie Street. At Toronto General Hospital, the second floor was set up as a diabetic ward. Soon, some of the most astounding happenings in the history of medical science were taking place there.

From this pioneer work, Banting and his colleagues learned a great deal. They found, for example, that even with insulin it was important for diabetics to stick to a diet. While patients could now eat normal quantities of food they still must be careful about their sugar intake.

They also learned about proper dosages and the danger signals of overdosage. They discovered that the best time for insulin injections was twenty minutes to half an hour before meals.

It soon turned out that insulin helped patients in other ways, too. Up to that time, diabetics had always been poor surgical risks, prone to various infections and gangrene. The outlook for women sufferers during childbirth was grim.

With insulin, however, all this changed. Operations could now be performed with no more than normal risk. Banting himself supervised the first successful amputation on an insulin patient. Now, too, the birth of a child to a woman diabetic was no longer fraught with danger and foreboding.

Until insulin, six out of every ten diabetics died of coma. And virtually every child with sugar sickness was doomed from the very start. Almost overnight the picture changed. The death rate began to drop sharply, and the life expectancy of diabetic patients skyrocketed.

With insulin injections, the parchment-dry skin of sufferers began to take on a healthy glow. Their eyes, traditionally dull and listless, grew bright and alert. With care, they could now eat and drink and participate in normal activities. In short, they could now look forward to leading useful lives of service—to themselves, their families and society.

The discovery of insulin received its first public announcement at a medical meeting in New Haven, Connecticut, late in 1922. Soon, word of the miracle was telegraphed to every corner of a thrilled and astonished world.

Banting and Best came down from Toronto with Macleod for the New Haven meeting. Banting was permitted to address the august gathering, but he was no public speaker at this time, and his talk, unfortunately, turned out to be a nervous, stumbling description of the work done by Best and himself. The distinguished physicians looked at this ill-at-ease young doctor and were far from impressed.

Then Macleod, as chairman of the meeting, got up and summarized the story of insulin smoothly and dramatically. He had attended hundreds of medical meetings and was an expert speaker at such gatherings.

The audience hung on his every word. Afterward, they gave him a thunderous ovation. Unfortunately, Professor Macleod failed to take the opportunity to set the record straight by pointing out that Banting and Best had made the discovery, not he.

Shortly afterward Macleod appeared at another medical gathering. This time it was before the American Association of Physicians, meeting in Chicago. They had asked him to appear to give a firsthand account of the momentous finding. Many of the leading doctors in America were present. They listened in hushed attention as Macleod outlined the details and significance of insulin treatment.

When he finished, a distinguished Chicago physician

arose. "I move that the association tender to Dr. Macleod and his associates a rising vote expressing its appreciation of his achievement," he declared. The motion was seconded and carried. "We are all agreed in congratulating Dr. Macleod and his collaborators on their miraculous achievement," a spokesman for the organization added as the entire membership rose to give the physiologist a standing ovation.

Again Macleod failed to clear the air. "I wish to thank the association very much in the name of my associates and myself," he replied. This statement merely compounded the misunderstanding, for it implied that Macleod was the leading figure in the discovery of insulin.

Actually it was never Macleod's intention to steal the credit rightly belonging to Banting and Best. In his younger days he had done work in German universities. There it was the tradition and practice for the director of a laboratory to announce new findings. In other words, the head of the laboratory always received the primary credit, regardless of who had actually conducted the research.

But in the more democratic atmosphere of the new world this was not done. It was considered unfair to the younger scientist who was struggling to gain a reputation.

No wonder, then, that Banting was infuriated when he realized what was happening. In view of Macleod's curious behavior he assumed that the older scientist was trying to reap the credit for the Banting and Best discovery. Many of Banting's close friends and associates, who knew the inside story of the work on insulin, felt the same way and were repelled by Macleod's actions.

Banting himself was not hungry for acclaim. Vanity was alien to him. Modesty and generosity were deeply ingrained characteristics. From his earliest days his parents had taught him that selfishness was a sin, and he constantly went out of his way to make it clear that Best was a codiscoverer.

In fact he did not even object to Macleod sharing in the recognition, for had it not been the older man who had agreed to make the facilities—meager as they were—available for the experiments? But he did resent bitterly what seemed to him a highhanded attempt to shut him and his young assistant out of the picture.

Fortunately, the true facts about the earth-shaking discovery began to appear in the press, as additional information was obtained, and the distorted early picture was corrected. Banting began to be hailed as the real discoverer with Best receiving credit as codiscoverer. Nevertheless he never forgave Macleod.

The clinical tests at Christie Street and at the Toronto General Hospital were astoundingly successful, more so than even Banting and Best had dared hope. The purpose, of course, was to give insulin a thorough trial before making it available to the general public. But even before the tests were completed, word spread about the miracles being performed in Toronto.

Soon from every country came gaunt, bone-weary pilgrims suffering from the sugar sickness. They poured into the city by ship, train, automobile and horse-and-buggy. Though Death hung over them like a specter, Hope and Faith brought them to Banting's door.

The "insulin rush" of 1922 turned out to be one of the most dramatic spectacles of the century.

As the supply of insulin increased, it was distributed to doctors wherever it was needed. Leading drug manufacturers in other countries were given the formula and permission to produce it.

Yet even after insulin was available outside of Toronto, diabetics continued to flock to that city. Many of them wanted Banting to treat them. Others came merely to see their benefactor and to thank him personally for the gift of life and hope he had given them. He was their prophet, and they came to do him homage.

In the beginning, Banting tried to explain that he was not in practice. He told the sufferers who asked him to treat them that other physicians were just as qualified to administer insulin once they had learned the proper technique. But it was of little avail. It was Dr. Banting they wanted and no one else.

Finally they won out. He was too kindhearted to turn them away, so he temporarily opened an office at 160 Bloor Street West, in Toronto. It was in dramatic contrast to the last time he had been in private practice in London when he had paced the floor morosely, hoping to see even a single patient.

Now long lines waited to see him each morning. In spite of this drain on his valuable time, he refused to charge anything but nominal fees. "Insulin doesn't belong to me," he explained to his fellow physicians simply. "It belongs to the world."

Once he was invited to address a group of medical students. "You must begin with an ideal and end with an ideal," he told them. "And if, by the wayside you falter, and place commerical gain before higher motives, you should stop your studies right now. Medicine is a profession of inspiration, perpetual and eternal."

Among the patients who journeyed long distances to be treated by Banting was the diabetic daughter of Charles

Evans Hughes, Chief Justice of the Supreme Court of the United States and a former candidate for the presidency. He was one of the most famous men in the world. Before long, Banting was able to control Miss Hughes's illness. Then he showed her how to use a hypodermic and inject insulin herself. This was another important development, for it made people less dependent on doctors, since the insulin had to be administered several times a day. They saw their doctors for periodic check-ups.

Another patient was a little boy named Jack Keightley. He was rushed from Johannesburg, South Africa, almost halfway around the world. He was very ill and there was great conjecture about his survival. A few weeks later the newspapers carried pictures of him engaged in a playful boxing match with his nurse.

Still another child, a little girl, arrived in Toronto too weak to walk. Within a few weeks she recovered so completely that she was able to put on a bathing suit and take a swim.

Such cases could be multiplied by the hundreds. Banting was overwhelmed by the gratitude of those he had been able to save from almost certain death, particularly the children. Gifts of every kind were showered upon him by individuals in all parts of the world. But it was the letters that touched him most deeply. These were his true reward, he felt.

One, from the small son of a physician in the United States, was typical. It read:

> Dear Dr. Banting,
>
> I am a diabetic and have had the disease for a little over two years. When I went to this particular clinic I had been getting 300 calories. I don't believe I would

have lived a month if I had not received insulin treatment. Now I am getting 1,800 calories. I have gained ten pounds and am still gaining. I am going to start school very soon.

Banting usually read his letters in private so that he could give way to his emotions without being seen. And often, particularly when the letters were from children, he found himself thinking of another child who used to run barefoot through the fields near Alliston many years ago—a little girl named Jane.

However, in those early days of insulin even Banting himself could not foresee the monumental impact his discovery would ultimately have on the future of mankind, both direct and indirect.

At Harvard University in Cambridge, Massachusetts, George R. Minot, a young physician, developed severe diabetes in 1921. As a doctor, Minot knew he was doomed. A few months later, however, Banting's miracle was announced to the world. Minot was given a new lease on life. A few years later, in 1926, Dr. Minot and William P. Murphy, a colleague, discovered a way to control another dread killer—pernicious anemia. Without insulin he might not have been alive to work on anemia, Minot himself declared.

Across the seas in England, diabetes had struck down a rising author. He began insulin treatment and soon was able to control the disease and go on with his writing. He lived to be eighty and became one of the greatest literary figures of the twentieth century—H. G. Wells.

In Austria a young Viennese physician Manfred Sakel heard about the amazing discovery. Soon he was using insulin on diabetic dope addicts in the psychiatric hospital where he was doing graduate work. One day he noticed that Banting's magic extract had a curiously calming effect on his patients, particularly when they were tense or excited.

Dr. Sakel began using insulin in connection with schizophrenia, the most hopeless of all mental illnesses. He put patients into a state of shock by using overdoses, then brought them out with glucose. The results he achieved were amazing. Seven out of ten who had recently contracted the mental disease were jolted back to reality and succeeded in making full recoveries. For the first time in medical history there was real hope for the mentally ill.

To make certain unscrupulous manufacturers would not profit from insulin and that it would be available at a fair price to everyone who needed it, Banting and his colleagues agreed to have the production process patented. The patent was taken out in the names of Banting, Best and Collip, since the latter had made an important contribution to the purification of the drug. But the rights were assigned to the University of Toronto.

Drug companies everywhere were now licensed to manufacture insulin without charge. The university's Connaught Laboratories were set up as a testing center. A nominal fee was charged for testing insulin made outside Canada. After the laboratories' expenses were paid, the rest of the fee was divided into two equal parts. One part went into an "Insulin Patent Pool" to maintain the patent rights and finance future research on the hormone. The second half was divided into three equal shares—to underwrite future research projects by the three patent holders: Banting, Best and Collip.

With patenting, it became possible to control the production of insulin so only reputable firms that adhere to the highest manufacturing standards would be licensed.

Not a cent of personal profit was made from insulin. The satisfaction of knowing that millions of lives would be saved through his discovery was reward enough, he insisted. Some years later, Sir William Mulock, chancellor of the University of Toronto, said of Banting with a chuckle: "He would give away his breeches. You didn't have to pick his pocket; he would freely give you the contents. No money sense, no money sense at all."

When Banting closed up his temporary office at 160 Bloor Street West, he added up his worldly assets—and found he was still four thousand dollars in debt to his father!

• CHAPTER NINE •

The World Hails a Hero

Overnight, Banting was catapulted to fame. He was suddenly a spectacular world figure. He was aghast at this new eminence, for it was something he had not foreseen even in his wildest dreams. After all, he had undertaken his great experiment out of sheer scientific curiosity and a desire to help others, not for personal glory. "Why did you do it?" he was asked time and again by newspaper reporters. "Because it was a problem that had to be solved," he replied.

Like most scientists, Banting was naïve about the ways of publicity. He had assumed that once the discovery was announced, it would be recognized in medical circles, and he would then be free to return quietly to other research problems. He was completely unprepared for the amazing popular reaction to insulin.

Now he learned that public opinion was a wondrous phenomenon, unlike anything he had ever experienced. One day he was an obscure, unsalaried researcher laboring in a tiny, ill-equipped laboratory; and the next he was being hailed as a popular hero who had ushered in a new age in medical research.

There were several important reasons for the spectacular impact of Banting's insulin discovery on the public. First, it had come with jarring suddenness. There had been no previous announcements or "progress reports" to cushion the surprise of the news. Many eminent scientists had been asserting for decades that diabetes was a "hopeless" disease. Expert researchers had devoted years to the problem, yet had failed to come up with a solution. The bulk of the public was convinced nothing could be done to control this dreaded illness.

Then, with no previous fanfare, the stunning announcement had been made that two young men, whom no one had ever heard about, had broken through the age-old barrier. Moreover, they had reached the goal with such speed and simplicity that the story had all the elements of superb drama.

Who was this mysterious Banting? Where did he come from? What made him tick as a scientist? These were questions that were on everyone's lips. After all, diabetes was not a rare disease that few persons cared about. It was one of the leading scourges of mankind.

Newspaper and magazine editors realized almost at once the bombshell impact of insulin. They knew it would touch the lives of untold millions, both the victims and the families and friends of the victims. Thus they put in motion the fascinating process that goes into the fashioning of a popular hero.

The press of the world began to hail Banting in bold headlines. The story of Banting and insulin was carried in every language. Long "human interest" articles appeared in the leading newspapers and magazines. Organizations began to shower him with honors. He was offered fabulous sums of money to lend his name and prestige to commercial enterprises—which he refused to do.

In Canada excitement reached fever pitch. Here was a young pioneer nation that had not yet developed an extensive reputation as a scientific center; yet it had given birth to one of the greatest medical discoveries of all time. So Banting became a new national hero.

The discoverer himself was embarrassed by it all. Naturally shy and modest, he never quite got used to the notion that he was a celebrity. He soon earned a reputation among newspaper reporters for being co-operative but completely self-effacing. He readily answered their questions about insulin and diabetes, for he wanted to make certain the public would not be given misinformation. But he was the bane of writers assigned to do "personality" stories about him because he was reluctant to talk about himself. For one thing, he could not for the life of him see why people should be interested in Fred Banting, the man. At the same time he feared that Best and the others would be overlooked, although they insisted that Banting was the real discoverer. "It's the insulin, not me, that's the important thing," Banting tried to tell the newspapermen who interviewed him. But they steadfastly refused to be convinced that the man who found insulin deserved to remain in anonymity. Consequently, much to Banting's chagrin, the articles continued to appear.

"The discoverer of insulin," one newspaper correspondent wrote, "almost gives the impression that a number of people were working on the problem and he happened to be around when the result was announced. . . . He is such a generous distributor that he hands away as much of the glory as he can."

Reporters kept after him night and day. Soon, all sorts of fantastic rumors began to appear in print. Banting was working on a cure for cancer, one newspaper said. Another claimed it had learned "on the highest authority" that he would soon announce the cause of heart disease. He was even credited with being close to the discovery of a vaccine for the common cold.

Official denials by Banting or the university did no good, of course. It merely added to the speculation. And the more he tried to avoid the limelight, the more persistent the newspapers became. They asked his opinion on all sorts of questions, including political and economic problems. When he refused to comment because he felt he was not qualified, the refusal itself became the subject of headlines! One day a reporter asked him a medical question that was so silly he shrugged it off. The next day the newspaper ran this headline:

DISCOVERER OF INSULIN RETREATS INTO SHELL AT ATTEMPTED INTERVIEW. REFRESHINGLY RUDE.

In spite of his trials and tribulations, Banting retained his sense of humor through it all. Once he was asked to address a meeting of the famous Canadian Club. He arose before the thousand assembled guests and held up the pancreas of a cow. "I don't want to interfere with your digestion," he declared with a straight face, "but if you want to know what insulin does, you have to understand the function of the pancreas." Whereupon he proceeded to give such a clear and simple explanation of his discovery that the audience of laymen arose and gave him a standing ovation.

Speechmaking always managed to unnerve him. No matter how often he spoke, he always felt uneasy before an audience. However, with practice he learned to deliver a talk without stumbling too badly. He had a gift for translating technical matters into simple language so that it was crystal clear to those who heard him. Nevertheless, one newspaper writer said that as a speaker "he reminds one of a little boy asked to recite something in front of a class when he wants to go swimming."

One evening Banting attended a banquet in honor of the hundredth anniversary of the birth of Louis Pasteur, the great French scientist. One after another, the speakers linked the name of Pasteur with Frederick Banting. Insulin was the greatest medical achievement since the discoveries credited to the immortal Frenchman, they pointed out. Before the night was over, the Pasteur banquet had turned into a Banting celebration. And throughout it all, Banting sat at a small table on the floor with the rest of the audience, largely unnoticed and shrinking with embarrassment!

Another time, while on the way home from Washington, D. C., he stopped overnight in Rochester, New York. As usual the newspapers managed to track him down and sent reporters to interview him at his hotel. The manager of the hotel was so moved by the presence of the guest that he refused to allow him to pay the bill. "I shall tell my visitors that Dr. Banting slept here," he explained. For the rest of the trip Banting debated with himself whether or not he should have insisted on paying the bill.

On the morning of February 11, 1923, Fred Banting came home to Alliston. A huge crowd was massed at the railroad depot. As the eleven twenty-five train chugged into the station and slowly braked to a stop, a great roar arose. Virtually the entire population of the town had turned out. In addition, the people had come from miles around—from the farms and neighboring towns and hamlets. These were

Banting's own people, and the pride showed itself in their eyes. Nothing like it had ever happened in those parts before, they told each other; for while Fred Banting was a hero of Canada, he was a son of Alliston.

With Banting that day was Charles Best. Together they were escorted to the Town Hall and seated on the platform near Banting's parents. The mayor presided at the public reception.

When Banting was introduced a roar went up that shook the hall. It lasted for a full five minutes. Finally the applause was quelled and a hushed silence hung over the audience as he began quietly to speak. He reminisced about his boyhood days in Alliston and the wonderful people whose friendship he valued so highly. Then he turned to face his parents. "It would never have been possible for me to undertake my research," he said in a voice touched with emotion, "had it not been for a man who has been right in your midst; and although during the past few years I have met many men and women, I have never yet met any finer or more self-sacrificing than my father and mother."

There was a moment's pause, and then the rafters trembled with a thunderous ovation. Finally Banting concluded his remarks with some wise words directed to the youngsters of Alliston. "Some say we have reached the limits of discovery," he declared. "They say there are no new fields to conquer. I don't believe that. There are still profitable fields for research, new things to find out. But nothing can be accomplished without hard work."

A few months later Banting was given the honor of opening the Canadian National Exhibition which was held in Toronto. His parents made the trip from Alliston to be present at the important occasion. Great crowds thronged around William and Margaret Banting to see the parents of Canada's favorite son and to congratulate them. Mrs. Banting had purchased a new pair of fine black gloves for the occasion. By day's end her right glove was worn clear through from shaking so many hands. Visitors and newspaper reporters asked her whether she was proud of her famous son. "Not proud, but thankful," she replied simply.

Now that Fate had touched a match to the Banting rocket, honors poured in from all over. He was awarded the Starr gold medal of the University of Toronto as well as the George Armstrong Peters prize for important contributions to surgical science. He also received the Reeve prize for the best piece of scientific research in the university's department of medicine and the Charles Mickle fellowship for having done the most during the preceding ten years to advance medicine. There were additional honors and medals from the United States, Scotland and England. But it was only the beginning. In the years to come he was to receive honorary degrees and major awards from many other leading universities and institutions throughout the world. Banting was never again to enjoy the anonymity of being a private citizen.

In 1923 he was appointed the first full professor of medical research in the history of the University of Toronto. The Chair was established through an annual grant of ten thousand dollars from the province of Ontario, and it was to be named after him. But Banting objected. He insisted that it be named in honor of Charles Best, too. The Ontario officials, now aware of Best's vital role, readily agreed to the request. The Chair was officially named the "Banting and Best Chair of Medical Research."

About this time, too, Sir Robert Falconer, president of

the University, and Chief Justice Sir William Mulock, the chancellor, decided to launch a great new project. The plan was to raise a minimum of five hundred thousand dollars to establish a Banting Research Foundation. The foundation would provide grants for medical research anywhere in Canada. It would thus encourage other obscure young Canadian scientists to continue the tradition started by Banting.

The plan caught fire. Contributions began to pour in, not only from Canada but from the citizens of other countries as well. The donations ranged all the way from the pennies of school children to checks of fifty thousand dollars from commercial firms. In a short time the goal was reached and the foundation was born.

What's more, gifts were made to the University of Toronto itself. Largely because of Banting's work at the university, the famous Rockefeller Foundation presented it with a gift of one million dollars as an endowment for the faculty of medicine. It now became clearer than ever that when the school of medicine had agreed to supply him with ten dogs and the use of a cramped laboratory and an unpaid assistant, it had made a gilt-edged investment.

Popular demands now began to grow for the Canadian government to give official recognition to Banting for his service to humanity and the honor he had brought to the nation. The Canadian Parliament thereupon passed a motion unprecedented in the Dominion's history. It provided an annual grant of seventy-five hundred dollars to the discoverer of insulin as an expression of the country's gratitude for his monumental achievement. The appropriation came just in the nick of time, for Banting was up to his ears in debt. It enabled him to repay the four thousand dollars he owed his father. "I have never known anything like the relief I felt when that was all paid back," he wrote later. "My father worked hard for it, and although what was his was ours, I didn't want to be owing it to him."

In the summer of 1923 Banting went to Europe to attend a series of scientific meetings. One was the British Medical Association Congress at Portsmouth, England. Throughout he sat unnoticed in the back of the hall. Just as at the Pasteur Centennial Banquet, the meeting soon turned into a Banting testimonial. But this time a distinguished physician Sir Thomas Horder recognized him. Amid a thunderous ovation he was escorted to the platform where he delivered a brief speech.

While in London Banting was urged by several fellow physicians to order a morning suit from a Bond Street tailor. He was perplexed by this sudden interest in his wardrobe and sensed conspiracy in the air. "Why?" he asked suspiciously.

"Don't ask questions," he was told. "You'll need it."

The English certainly go in for formality, he told himself. However, he ordered the suit.

At ten minutes to five one evening he received an urgent message. It was an order commanding him to appear at Buckingham Palace the following morning at eleven o'clock for an interview with His Majesty, the King! The reason for ordering a morning suit now became quite clear.

Later that evening the Canadian High Commissioner paid him a visit. He took the still-amazed Banting in tow and rushed him around London to buy a hat, gloves and a cane. The following morning Banting taxied to Buckingham Palace at the appointed time, feeling self-conscious in his formal attire. He was ushered through the palace and finally ended up in a huge, magnificently furnished room. There he was introduced to George V.

Left alone behind closed doors, the former farm lad from Alliston and His Majesty were soon chatting together easily. The king was a cultured and educated gentleman. He asked Banting intelligent questions about insulin and his own background. They also discussed Canada and the progress of medical science. The conversation soon became so absorbing the young scientist was allowed to stay long past the time alloted for the interview. Later he reported how surprised he was to find King George so well versed in medical affairs. "When I mentioned a hospital in London," he told friends, "I was amazed to find the king knew in pounds, shillings and pence what it cost to run that hospital. So many pounds in 1900, so many pounds in 1910 and so on."

All in all, 1923 was an exciting year for Banting. But the dramatic high point came with a momentous announcement from Stockholm, Sweden. It stated that Drs. Macleod and Banting had been named to share the coveted Nobel prize in medicine as "codiscoverers of insulin." The award of forty thousand dollars was to be divided equally.

When the announcement reached Banting, his reaction was mixed. As a researcher he was proud and gratified that his work was deemed significant enough to earn the most important distinction in the world of science. Yet he was bitter, too.

To Banting and others who knew the inside story of insulin, the action of Sweden's Caroline Institute in naming Macleod the codiscoverer was a glaring blunder. The fact that Macleod's name had been listed first in the official announcement compounded the error. It was all the result of the older scientist's failure to clear up the initial misunderstand surrounding the announcement of the discovery. This naturally added fuel to Banting's indignation.

He did not object to Macleod's sharing in the honors, but the fact that Best had been overlooked outraged his sense of justice. Always devastatingly honest with himself and others, he recalled with bitterness that it was Charles Best who had sweated with him in the grimy little laboratory during the long steaming summer—not Macleod. Macleod had been in Europe on vacation. It was Best who had shared with him the meager meals cooked over a Bunsen burner. And it was Best who had prowled the streets with him searching for dog owners who would sell them animals for their experiments. Now that they had succeeded in doing what they had started out to do, was Best to be forgotten?

Banting made up his mind to have none of it. His reaction was instinctive. And it was typical. He would refuse the Nobel prize as a protest against a gross injustice!

However, his close friends managed to cool him off. They argued that it would be a pointless gesture and everyone would lose by it. After all, the winning of a Nobel prize was a magnificent triumph for a Canadian. It was a great victory for the nation regardless of who won it. National as well as individual pride was involved. It would spur other young Canadians to go into scientific research. And in years to come, the controversy would be forgotten but the important fact would remain in the record—the fact that the Nobel prize in medicine for 1923 had gone to Canada.

Banting agreed—reluctantly. His sense of patriotism and devotion to the cause of future Canadian science won out.

He would accept the Nobel prize. But he insisted on having the order of the names changed to read "Banting and Macleod." Then he performed an act that today stands as one of the most generous in the history of science. He sent a message to Charles Best informing him that he would share his twenty thousand-dollar portion of the prize with him and issued a public statement to that effect.

To make doubly certain that Best would receive due recognition, he dispatched a telegram to Dr. Eliot P. Joslin, the chairman of a meeting at Harvard University Medical School in Boston where Best was addressing the medical students. The telegram read:

> AT ANY MEETING OR DINNER PLEASE READ FOLLOWING: I ASCRIBE TO BEST EQUAL SHARE IN THE DISCOVERY. HURT THAT HE IS NOT SO ACKNOWLEDGED BY NOBEL TRUSTEES. WILL SHARE WITH HIM.
>
> BANTING

When this message was read before the assembled guests, the applause was overwhelming, not only for Banting's generous gesture but in recognition of his young associate and partner.

Following Banting's announcement, Professor Macleod decided to divide his share with Dr. Collip. Best remained at the University of Toronto where he continued his research activities in other areas, and entered medical school.

Then on June 4, 1925, another interesting bit of news broke—Frederick Banting and Marion Robertson were married.

He was then thirty-three years old and a confirmed bachelor—or so everyone thought. For years Mrs. O'Neil had been urging him to "find yourself a nice girl, one who will look after you." He had managed to resist for a time. But finally she won out. It was a victory she considered almost as monumental as the discovery of insulin.

The romance was set in motion during the period that insulin was being tested on the second floor of Toronto General Hospital. One day Banting wandered into the radiology department—and came face to face with the pretty young technician he had first met in 1919 shortly before his discharge from the Army at the Christie Street Hospital. They recognized each other at once. He asked for a date and Marion nodded smilingly. That was how it began.

Soon they were seeing a great deal of each other. Aside from Mrs. O'Neil who divined the secret without being told, few of his friends knew of the budding romance.

The wedding, a simple, tasteful ceremony, was held in the home of the bride's uncle Dr. James Caven. Only the members of the immediate family were present. They left on their honeymoon by car, a shiny new roadster. The automobile, a far cry from the rattly old secondhand Ford, was one of the few luxuries Banting had permitted himself.

They drove to Atlantic City and then to New Haven, Connecticut, where Yale University awarded the groom an honorary doctor of science degree. From there they went to New York City. Wherever they went they were entertained royally, often by the families of diabetes victims whom Banting had treated in Toronto.

On the twelfth of July they set sail for a grand tour of the Caribbean. Banting had been invited to deliver a paper on insulin at the International Conference on Health Problems in Tropical America, which was scheduled to be held in Kingston, Jamaica. When the United Fruit Company heard of his acceptance it invited the distinguished scientist and his new bride to be its guests on a company ship that would take them on a cruise to all its Caribbean ports. Banting and Marion were excited at the thought of a tropical honeymoon and gratefully accepted the offer.

The trip took two months. It was a delightful experience that gave Banting an opportunity to relax for the first time in years and also to resume his painting.

When they returned to Toronto they plunged eagerly into the task of planning and supervising the construction of their new home. It was to be an attractive, solidly built structure not far from the laboratory in the Pathology Building of the medical school which now served Banting as headquarters.

The following year, 1925, the Bantings toured Europe. In Stockholm, Sweden, he delivered his Nobel prize address which is required of all award winners. Wherever they went they stayed in small, unpretentious hotels in order to save money and avoid publicity. But the attempt to remain anonymous was of no avail. Banting's name was so well known that it was recognized no matter where they traveled. "Banting" and "insulin" were magic passwords that dissolved barriers of language and custom.

In 1926 there was a trip to the Canadian West to attend the annual convention of the Canadian Medical Association in Victoria. It was a repeat of the triumphal European tour. From the primitive towns and backwoods settlements prospectors, traders and dirt farmers poured forth to meet them. They extended their leathery, work-toughened hands eagerly for a chance to shake the hand of Canada's greatest medical hero.

In much of the wild country over which they were travel

ing there were no physicians. On a number of occasions Banting was summoned from the hotel or train to give emergency treatment or advice. In spite of the inconvenience to himself and Marion, he gave his services freely and graciously. Once he was summoned by a constable to the bedside of a dying old prospector. The policeman was apologetic. "I know it's a big imposition calling you out like this, sir," he said. "And if old Hank weren't in such a bad way I would never have done it. After all, you're an important man in Canada."

Banting reassured him. "There's no need to apologize," he replied. "I hope I never become so important as to forget that I'm first of all a doctor."

There was little to be done for the impoverished old man. He gave what emergency treatment he could, however, and asked to be kept informed of the patient's condition. By the time the train arrived at the next stop there was a telegram saying that the prospector had died. The message saddened Banting. As a boy he had read the exciting stories of the old pioneer days with great relish. It was an interest that had stayed with him even after he reached manhood. With the death of the obscure old frontiersman he felt that a colorful bit of the old West had died with him.

Another time a young, unconscious girl was brought to the hotel where the Bantings were staying. He recognized her at once as one of his early diabetes patients. He learned that she had missed her lunch to go horseback riding and had developed insulin shock. Immediately he treated her with glucose—in spite of the girl's nurse who protested loudly that her patient was a diabetic and must not be given sugar under any circumstances!

The girl soon recovered to find the familiar face of her

old physician staring down at her. As soon as she got over her initial amazement, she threw her arms around Banting in a tearful reunion.

Many men, having once made a contribution as monumental as the discovery of insulin, might have been content to spend the rest of their lives basking in the glory of this single achievement. Not Frederick Banting. Fame had made certain demands on him, and these he had fulfilled. But he never managed to feel quite comfortable in the role of popular hero.

Now he began to grow increasingly restive. He was impatient to return to the laboratory, anxious to resume the quiet life of a medical researcher once more. After all, he was primarily a scientist, he told himself, and as long as there were unknown frontiers in science still to be explored, a scientist's place was in his laboratory . . .

• *CHAPTER TEN* •

The Peaceful Years

The quiet years had begun. They were to be years marked by hard, satisfying work. Banting had a small staff to assist him now. It consisted of a briskly efficient secretary and assistant Sadie Gairns, and a laboratory technician. In addition he was assigned two graduate fellows to work with him on research projects.

Headquarters was a cramped suite of three rooms. There was an office adjoined by an animal room and a laboratory. Many scientists would have considered it a meager setup for a researcher with Banting's distinguished reputation.

Banting, however, was delighted with it. It was a thousand times superior to the now famous laboratory bench that had served as the birthplace of insulin. Though cluttered and dusty it was busy as a behive most of the time. It had an air of intimacy that gave him the feeling of being at home. For most of all, he dreaded pompous formality. It stifled his thinking, he claimed. Some years later, after moving to magnificent new quarters, he complained wryly: "The one thing I dread is affluence. I have a lovely office now, with pictures on the wall and a swivel chair, and I can't do anything."

One day he delivered a speech before a medical fraternity. "Marble desks, cushioned chairs and suites of rooms in buildings of fine architecture are not the essentials of research," he stated. "I sometimes think they detract from its true spirit. Pasteur and Bernard worked in a cellar." And while he did not mention it, he might have added that Fred Banting and Charles Best had worked in a stifling attic.

He shunned personal affectation for the same reason. Dressed-up dinners and stuffy receptions bored him to tears. He survived such occasions by occupying the time caricaturing long-winded speakers on the sides of menus or program cards.

"No one has ever had an idea in a dress suit," he once said. Another time, in 1930, he confessed to a friend that he was still wearing the dress suit he had bought in 1919. "It was my first and only dress suit," he explained. "I bought it secondhand then for twenty-five dollars. It was made five years before that. My wife hates it but it is still a good suit—fine old prewar cloth."

Banting's scientific interest began to range far and wide about this time. His curiosity was boundless. He poked his longish nose into everything. He and his assistants did extensive work in cancer and the chemical treatment of mental disorders, an interest stimulated in part by Manfred Sakel's work with insulin on schizophrenics. He even investigated the nutritional properties of royal jelly, the mysterious food of the queen honey bee!

One of his most important contributions was in the field of silicosis research. Silicosis is a disease of the lungs. It is contracted mostly by miners, especially those working in gold mines where the blasting, drilling and crushing fills the air with quartz dust. The symptoms are short breath, wheezes and a racking cough that never goes away. These symptoms are caused by a hardening of the tissue in the lungs, known as fibrosis. Often the disease becomes so bad the miner suffers complete disability.

Quite by accident, in 1927, Banting first became interested in silicosis. On the faculty of the University of Toronto was a professor of mining engineering named H. E. T. Haultain. One day Banting found he had need of a new piece of laboratory equipment—a high-speed centrifuge. It was not unlike some of the machines used in mining. He called on Professor Haultain to help him design the centrifuge.

Always curious to learn new things about other fields of work, he began to have long talks with the mining expert about conditions in the mines. Lung disease was one of the thorniest problems, he learned; particularly silicosis, the dread of every miner. It was exacting a tragic toll of human life each year. Furthermore, it cost governments many millions of dollars a year in welfare and disability compensation.

Banting decided to attack the disease boldly and directly, as he had done in the case of diabetes. He began to read everything he could lay his hands on in the medical libraries. He also tried to learn as much as he could about mining operations. Soon he knew a great deal about silicosis and the work done on it by researchers in the past.

He assigned a team of researchers to go down to the mines and find out how miners live and work. They were to co-operate with the mine owners and supervisors who were also vitally concerned in tracking down the cause of the malady. "I want you to feel, taste and smell the dust that produces silicosis," Banting instructed his investigators.

The task of tracing mine dust was not an easy one. It was a long, grueling business. The techniques used to measure dust contents were primitive. The mines were dirty, dark and cramped in terms of working space, and conditions could not be controlled as in a laboratory.

Soon, however, Banting's team learned many things that were not known before. They developed improved ways of measuring the concentration and identifying the components that make up dust. Samples of mine dust were taken and used on experimental animals to find out how tissues react to the tiny particles of minerals that constantly float around in the air miners breathe.

The attack was a full-scale one. Banting decided to spare no effort to lick this terrible disease. This time he had a great advantage he did not have during the diabetes experiments. He was now a distinguished scientist and his voice carried a good deal of weight at the university. He was thus able to call on other departments to co-operate in the project. These included the department of physics which helped a great deal in devising equipment and the department of mineralogy whose members had an expert knowledge of metals.

After many months the mineral silica, which is known chemically as silicon dioxide, was found to be the culprit in silicosis. The researchers immediately concluded that it was the puncturing action of the tiny, sharp silica dust particles that caused the lung damage.

But further experiments showed that this was not true. They learned that fibrosis, or the hardening of lung tissue, was caused by chemical action. When silica was dissolved in the lung tissue fluid, silicic acid was formed. It was the irritating action of this acid that damage the cells of the lungs.

Banting decided that if a way could be found to prevent

the formation of silicic acid it might be the solution to the problem of how to prevent silicosis. Accordingly, he called a meeting in his office. It was attended by the members of his research team and experts from the mines themselves. Numerous suggestions were made, discussed and discarded. The answer that came to mind almost at once was the possibility of filtering the air so no silica dust would enter the lungs in the first place. This idea was ruled out because filtering would be prohibitive in cost, and efficient equipment had not been developed for such a purpose.

Eventually the discussion centered about ways to combat silicic acid by chemical means. Banting was in his element here, for the problem was similar to the one he faced years ago in finding a way chemically to neutralize the damaging effect of powerful pancreatic digestive juice in the production of insulin. He put the problem squarely. "It seems there is no practical way to keep silica out of the lungs, gentlemen," he declared. "So we must think in terms of an antidote—some chemical agent that will neutralize the silica after it has entered the lungs." The investigators agreed to try this approach.

For many months they waged the campaign to locate an antidotal dust. Many different minerals were tried. The failures mounted. Then one day the researchers came to Banting with an encouraging report. While conducting experiments at the mine they had tried metallic aluminum powder and found it prevented silica from turning into silicic acid. It was a startling discovery, and Banting was jubilant. This, he decided, might prove to be just the antidote they were seeking.

He urged immediate clinical tests. A mill was devised to grind and crush aluminum into fine dust and disperse it in the air. A program of therapy was started at the McIntyre Mine in Ontario. In a few short months it was clear that the treatment was a success. The test findings showed that for the first time in history it was possible to prevent silicosis in human beings. Thus the way had been paved to save hundreds of thousands of lives.

Soon the first medical report on the revolutionary treatment was ready to be announced to the world. It was to be presented at a special meeting of the Toronto Academy of Medicine. Banting's researchers pleaded with him to deliver the paper personally. But he steadfastly refused and insisted that they do it.

This action was typical of him. Although he had initiated, organized and encouraged the project all the way, the actual work had been carried out by his subordinates. He decided, therefore, that if he were now to make the report, people might assume he had performed the experiments with "his own two hands." It was much more important to him that the young scientists in his department get the lion's share of the credit instead. The unfortunate episode with Macleod was still vivid in his mind. And he made up his mind never to be guilty of doing to others what Macleod had done to him.

Nevertheless, when the paper was read at the medical meeting and reported in the world press the magic of Banting's name dominated the newspaper articles. He was furious at this turn of events, but his assistants were delighted. They felt he had been the guiding spirit all along and deserved the credit in spite of himself. "It's our honor to be associated with you in the public mind," they told him.

Speech requests began pouring in from all over. Banting turned them down. One was from an organization in the

United States. He sent a telegram of refusal, explaining that his role in the silicosis research had been a secondary one. But the spokesman for the group was persistent. He telephoned Banting hoping to convince him to change his mind. With characteristic stubbornness, the scientist refused a second time. But he offered to ask one of the men who had actually done the work to speak instead.

"My organization wouldn't go along with that, Dr. Banting," said the voice on the other end of the line. "We want you or no one."

Banting was infuriated. "What you want is not a speech on silicosis but an exhibition of Frederick Banting," he retorted, trying to maintain his self-control. "I'm sorry, but I'm not on exhibit."

More and more of his time was now devoted to guiding and encouraging the younger researchers under his wing. He firmly believed that a scientist's most important piece of equipment is his ability to think independently. And he had a quiet genius for stimulating them to think for themselves.

The technique he developed was simple and direct. He asked questions, a great many questions. His subordinates learned that before they could give answers that would satisfy their chief they first had to clarify the problem in their own minds. Banting was convinced it was the most effective teaching method ever devised.

He couldn't stand scientific jargon. He believed that the use of complicated technical terms was a sign that the researcher hadn't taken the trouble to think out the matter clearly. Very often a subordinate during a conference lost himself in long, confusing words. When this happened, Banting leaned back in his chair, puffed away at his pipe or cigarette and stared silently at the ceiling. Inevitably the young scientist found himself enmeshed in a web of technical jargon from which there was no escape. Then Banting stepped in.

"Just a minute," he interrupted with a mystified expression. "Would you tell me what you're talking about? You lost me way back, and I have the feeling you've lost yourself, too."

The bluntness of the statement jolted the speaker into silence. Then Banting added more gently, "Remember, I don't know much about this problem you're discussing. The moment you started throwing those big textbook words around I was thoroughly confused. Let's try putting it into simple English."

The speaker then succeeded in boiling the matter down to two or three simple sentences. "Now that's more like it," Banting retorted with an approving grin. "Why didn't you say it that way in the first place?"

The ability to strip away the nonessentials and get to the heart of a problem was the key to Banting's success as a teacher. Young researchers sometimes resented this down-to-earth approach. They didn't relish the idea of being forced to admit they had been guilty of muddled thinking. But after a short time they came to realize the soundness of such training.

One young investigator who was with Banting for a time was Dr. Jean McNamara, an Australian doctor who later did important research in polio. She had worked at laboratories in the United States before coming to Toronto. Her enthusiasm for Banting's scientific approach was unbounded. "I thank heaven that there is one place in the world where complicated things are made simple instead of simple things being made complicated," she remarked to a fellow scientist.

Banting's mechanical aptitude was superb. He had a genius for devising emergency apparatus and techniques during experiments. It was one of the main reasons he had been able to discover insulin where everyone else had failed. And as in other matters, he firmly believed laboratory gadgets should be kept simple.

If an assistant worked out a mechanism that would require several skilled workmen for three days and would cost several hundred dollars to build, Banting usually came up with a substitute. Sometimes it looked clumsy, consisting of a strange assortment of spare beakers, surplus rubber hose or other items that happened to be lying around. Yet curiously enough, the spur-of-the-moment setup usually worked.

"It's not that I begrudge you the money," Banting explained apologetically. "But if it will accomplish the same purpose, why not spend ten dollars instead of two hundred? You can buy a lot of laboratory animals for a hundred and ninety dollars!"

A good deal of his time was given to cancer research. He had been interested in finding a cure for this dreaded killer ever since his interview with King George V. At that time His Majesty had suggested that Banting put his talents to work on the problem.

The discoverer of insulin did not succeed in finding such a cure. But the hundreds of experiments he conducted on mice and chickens made an important contribution by ruling out many of the cancer theories advanced by medical scientists in the past.

In spite of the long hours in the laboratory, Banting

found time for his family. In 1929 his only son William Robertson Banting was born. He had always loved children. Now with a child of his own his joy was boundless. He was deeply devoted to little Bill and spent every spare moment with him.

His gift for storytelling was put to good use. Night after night he entertained his son with bedtime yarns. At one time he even thought about gathering together these original tales in a children's book.

On Bill's second birthday, Banting found himself in Quebec on an important matter. He was lonesome for the little boy and set down some meditations concerning his son's future in his diary.

"I hope his young life will be sunshine, but he will have clouds and storms and mists," he wrote. "Above all, I hope his life will be useful . . . After all, work is the only thing in life that brings happiness."

Painting continued to remain Banting's lifelong hobby. He had put his brushes away during the long, weary months of work on insulin. Afterward, however, he had picked them up again permanently and even started a modest art collection.

With the announcement of insulin his classmates in "Meds Seventeen" got together and commissioned the famous Canadian artist Curtis Williamson to paint Banting's portrait. During the long hours of sitting, he put the time to good use by asking the artist questions about brush technique, mixing paints and composition. In this manner he learned a great deal that he had missed by never having had formal art training.

Banting soon joined the Arts and Letters Club of Toronto, and there he met a number of important artists who were having a great deal of influence on Canadian art. One of the most distinguished was A. Y. Jackson, a brilliant landscape painter. One day Banting visited his studio to buy one of his pictures. It was the start of a warm, permanent friendship.

Both were simple, modest men who wore their fame gracefully. They enjoyed the outdoors and exploring the mysteries of nature. Together they began to take sketching and painting trips. It became an annual affair. Each year they went to a virgin part of Canada to paint the beauties of their native land. Banting learned a great deal about landscape painting from Jackson.

Since boyhood Banting had dreamed of exploring the little-known parts of the world, including the Arctic. Now a superb opportunity presented itself. Jackson was scheduled to sail aboard the steamer *Beothic* on a tour of Royal Canadian Mounted Police stations in the Far North. He was to serve as official artist for the expedition. "Wouldn't it be wonderful if you could come along?" he said to Banting.

"Maybe I can arrange it," Banting replied.

He asked government officials for permission. They saw it as a golden opportunity. For some years there had been a pressing need for a survey of health and social conditions among the Eskimos. But there had been no qualified expert available or willing to endure the hardships of such a trip. Banting's request came along at just the right time, and he agreed to make the study.

The expedition braved violent storms, freezing weather and a multitude of discomforts, but it was an exciting adventure. The ship churned its dangerous way up to Ellesmere Island, the most northerly settlement in the world. Banting saw icebergs along the shore and great snow-covered mountains. They plowed through a sea of fantastic islands of floating ice inhabited by herds of sunning walrus and seal. Jackson and he set up their easels in the center of quaint little Eskimo villages swarming with excited children and barking husky dogs. They painted majestic peaks crowned with pure-white snow. They visited Eskimo families in their curious little houses banked with sod. Banting asked many questions, and he took endless notes on Eskimo life.

Later, these facts were incorporated into his report to the government. The report concluded that poverty and ignorance coupled with official apathy had been exacting a terrible toll in human health and human life among the Eskimos. It recommended that a program of medical aid be instituted to help this unfortunate people, a recommendation that eventually was carried out by the Canadian government.

Banting's style of painting reflected the vigor and color of his personality. It showed his bold, strong-willed approach to life. Most of his works were landscapes, although one newspaper art critic, in reviewing his work, wondered why the discoverer of insulin should choose to put scenery rather than dogs on canvas! Years later, a number of his pictures painted during the *Beothic* expedition were included in an exhibit of two hundred of his works at the Toronto Art Gallery. The display also showed his sketches and wood carvings, another of his hobbies.

The Banting and Best department of medical research, headed by Banting, was bursting at the seams. Additional research space was also needed by the departments of pathology, pathological chemistry and bacteriology. The clinical laboratories of the university were ready to expand, too.

A joint project was thus undertaken by the University of Toronto and the government of Canada. The plan was to erect a research center to be known as the Banting Research Institute. The architects' plans called for a six-story Georgian-style building of reinforced steel and concrete, with an exterior of red brick and stone trim.

The formal opening and dedication of the institute was set for September 16, 1930. To mark the occasion, elaborate ceremonies were planned. It was to be attended by representatives of thirty leading universities in Canada, Great Britain and the United States.

Suddenly, a few days before the official opening, Banting took sick. He was doubled over with severe stomach pains. A fellow physician Dr. G. W. Ross examined him and diagnosed it as acute appendicitis. Immediate surgery was indicated.

But with characteristic stubbornness, Banting refused to agree to the appendectomy. He was concerned about those who were planning the dedication. He knew it was too late to call it off. And while he personally cared little about the formal honors planned for him, he knew the glittering ceremony meant much to the university. A number of distinguished scientists were traveling across the ocean to attend. As the central figure his absence would dampen the day's events. The operation would have to be postponed, he insisted to his physician colleagues, in spite of their strongest protests.

So Banting attended the academic ceremonies. They were among the most colorful in the university's history. The faculties and famous guests were dressed in impressive academic robes. The main speaker was Lord Moynihan, president of the Royal College of Surgeons. He had come from Leeds, England, to deliver his address.

"Banting has conquered," he told the solemn audience, "and today, as a gift from all mankind, he wears with so becoming humility the crown of immortality. In his honor we raise today this temple of science."

Newspaper correspondents from papers throughout Canada and from many foreign lands were on hand. Their articles were full of warmth and affection for this modest genius who, after eight years of international renown, still managed to wear the mantle of fame with quiet dignity. One writer noted that Banting looked "like a small boy who has been caught stealing jam."

Many of his friends and relatives were asked to give statements for publication. One of these was Mrs. O'Neil. "I am proud to know the young man the Banting Institute is named for," she said beaming. When Banting was told about her remark, he replied, "My father's name would grace any building."

The following week, he successfully underwent the delayed appendectomy, satisfied that he had not disappointed the university officials who had counted on him.

But the quiet happiness of those peaceful years was marred by personal sorrow. He and Marion were not getting along. This became increasingly clear as time passed. Their marriage which had been so perfect at the outset entered dark days. The deepening incompatibility continued to fester. And in 1932 the marriage ended in divorce. It had lasted for eight years.

Because of the respect and affection for Banting among members of the press, the newspapers agreed to "play down" the divorce proceedings, although normally a name as famous as his would have provided grist for the headline writers. The newspaper editors agreed among themselves to limit coverage to a brief, factual announcement. But one newspaper with a reputation for scandalmongering broke the agreement. It gave sensational treatment to the story. This automatically released the other papers. Soon the divorce was headlined throughout Canada.

The publicity added another dimension of grief to Banting's deepening sorrow. He became moody and seclusive. He stopped attending meetings of the Arts and Letters Club and stayed away from his favorite restaurants. It was a time of sadness and soul searching. He asked himself: Why had the marriage failed? What had he done wrong? But for once he could not find an answer. This was one problem for which science could supply no explanation.

Forlorn, guilt ridden, Banting turned once again to the only cure he knew for unhappiness: hard work. Soon his involvement in important scientific tasks succeeded in taking his attention away from his personal sorrows. Moreover, he had been given custody of little Bill, and this helped brighten his outlook for the future.

Little by little he resumed his social life where he had left off. He began to accept the invitations of friends to visit their homes and entertained them in the little apartment he had rented. The Arts and Letters Club, as well as other places he used to visit regularly, began to see more and more of him again as time went by.

One day in 1934 an important announcement was carried in the press. In recognition of his great service to science and humanity, the British Empire would confer a knighthood on Banting, the statement said.

That June he made the trip to Ottawa for the colorful ceremony of investiture. The leading officials of the nation were present. As Banting knelt before the throne, the governor general of Canada touched him upon the shoulder with a sword. With that act he was created a "Knight Commander of the Civil Division of the Order of the British Empire."

A few moments later, he rose to his feet and the ribbon and badge of knighthood were placed about his neck. He was now *Sir* Frederick Banting!

For a brief moment it seemed to Banting that he had come a long way from the modest farm near Alliston. Then he thought of his father and mother—and it came to him suddenly that the honor conferred on him that day belonged to them, too. He knew, then, that the farm with its green fields and rolling hills wasn't so far away after all.

• CHAPTER ELEVEN •

Warrior Against Death

The peaceful years were coming to an end. By the middle of the thirties the ugly rumblings of a new barbarianism were beginning to be heard throughout the world. In Germany Nazi jack boots clattered along the cobbled streets. Throughout Italy the black shirts of fascism were a common sight. And in Russia the red flag of communism held ominous sway.

Most people closed their ears and eyes to the gathering storm. The few who heard and saw and were troubled by it tried to warn the rest. But their words were ignored, for the people of the democracies were not yet ready to accept the truth about the totalitarian threat.

One of the early prophets was Banting. All during the period of democratic indifference and complacency he remained clear sighted and antitotalitarian. He was deeply concerned about the future, and felt that unless the democratic nations opened their eyes the ideal of human freedom and decency in which he believed so strongly was in grave danger.

In 1935 he made a trip to Russia. It was to attend the International Physiological Congress which was to meet in Leningrad and Moscow that year. The president of the congress was Ivan Petrovitch Pavlov who at eighty-six was one of the world's most famous physiologists and the scientist who had originated the concept of the "conditioned reflex."

Banting used the opportunity to see as much as possible of the Soviet Union. He had heard a great deal about communist Russia, and as a scientist he was eager and curious to dig out the facts for himself. His visa was good for two weeks, and at the end of that time he applied for a two-week extension. The minor official to whom he applied refused to grant the request. He feared that Banting was a foreign agent intent on spying. Finally, Banting pulled out a photograph showing himself with Professor Pavlov. The passport official took one look and beamed. "Anyone who knows the great academician Ivan Petrovitch Pavlov is to be treated with the greatest respect," he said as he stamped the visa and handed it back.

Banting was astounded that the ordinary man-in-the-street in Russia should be able to recognize a picture of a scientist and treat him with the respect reserved for a movie star or athletic hero in his own country. It taught him an important lesson.

"Until science and scientists in the democratic nations are deemed worthy of the respect accorded them in Russia," he told his fellow scientists after his return, "we are in grave danger of surrendering our future without a fight."

During his Russian tour he went everywhere—visiting farms, factories and laboratories. He asked many questions and took a great many notes. Like all distinguished visitors he was given the "official tour." But fearing that in this way he would see only what the Russians wanted him to see, he made it a practice to slip away on his own. Also, he changed his accommodations from first to second class in order to see how the ordinary Russian lived. When the Russian officials learned of this they were amazed that he was willing to give up the ease and comfort of choice accommodations, although he tried in vain to explain the reason to them.

Banting was greatly impressed by the strides made by the communists in bettering conditions. He was particularly interested in the emphasis on science and education. Of course, he was under no illusions as to the true nature of communism. But as a scientist, he was first of all a realist. He realized it was important for freedom-loving nations to know the facts, for unless they learned about true conditions in Russia and were aroused to action, there was a real danger they would be overtaken scientifically and industrially in future years.

When Banting returned to Canada he tried desperately to make his findings known. He wrote articles for magazines and gave interviews to newspapers. The democracies' conception of the Russians was all wrong, he warned. Contrary to popular belief the Soviet Union was not a semi-barbaric nation governed by comic opera commissars. The rulers of Russia, he declared, were tough, shrewd leaders who put their faith and the future of their country in science and education.

"No people in the world so fully realize that the science of today is the research of yesterday, and the research of today is the science of tomorrow," he wrote in one article. "Today, scientific research and the application of science to industry and agriculture is the most impressive activity in the Soviet Union. There is no country in the world that is progressing so rapidly in this regard."

Now Banting was no wild-eyed radical. In politics he classified himself as a conservative. But regardless of his own political beliefs, he felt that honesty compelled him to report what he had actually seen, not what people wanted to believe. It took a great deal of courage. His warnings, however, made little dent on the public mind. For the truth was that people were in no mood to listen. Banting's statements were so at variance with accepted beliefs that few persons took him seriously.

In fact it took twenty-two years for events to bear out the uncanny accuracy of his reports on the progress of Soviet science. It was not until 1957, when Russian scientists hurtled the world's first earth satellite into outer space, that Banting's early warnings took on full significance.

Fortunately his efforts to awaken his countrymen were not a total loss. Somewhere high in Canadian government circles a few farsighted officials weighed his statements carefully. "Perhaps Sir Frederick has a point," said one. "Maybe it's true that at the present rate the totalitarian nations will outstrip us in science in a few years," added another.

Because of Banting's experience in research matters and his deep interest in spurring greater scientific effort, he received an appointment to the National Research Council of Canada. It proved to be a vital step in safeguarding the nation's future.

Banting hated all forms of totalitarianism. He was particularly repelled by the Nazis and their anti-Semitism. He considered Hitler's Germany the most immediate threat to the future of the democratic world. Many refugee scientists began to flock to Toronto in the hope of working at the Banting Institute. There they received sympathy and encouragement.

One of these scientists was Dr. Bruno Mendel, a German cancer expert of the Jewish faith. Although he had never met Banting, he knew of his great reputation. Sir Frederick greeted him warmly and asked many questions about his work and his experience in Germany under Hitler. Dr. Mendel was amazed to find out how much Banting already knew about Nazi aims and methods. Years later he wrote that Banting "was one of the very few of my acquaintances here who saw the folly of 'peace in our time' on Nazi terms."

Sir Frederick went out of his way to make the refugee scientist and his family feel at home in a strange land. A few minutes after their first interview ended, Mrs. Mendel received a call at the hotel where the family was staying temporarily. It was Banting telephoning to invite the Mendel family, including the children, to have dinner with him at his favorite restaurant that evening.

Promptly at seven Dr. and Mrs. Mendel and the youngsters found the discoverer of insulin waiting in the lobby of the hotel. A friend was with him. He was a well-known Canadian, a Jew, whom Banting had invited in order to put the refugee family at ease by showing them that they were no longer in Germany where Jews were considered an inferior race.

Dr. Mendel was put to work at the Banting Institute at once. In the years that followed, he and Banting became close friends. When the British appeased Hitler at Munich by agreeing to sell out Czechoslovakia, Banting was deeply ashamed of the treaty. "Our people think we are buying peace," he told Dr. Mendel. "But we're not. We're postponing the day of reckoning. And the more we put it off, the more it will cost us. Let's all get ready for war."

For the same reason he openly supported the democratic government of Spain against the fascist rebel army when the bloody Spanish Civil War broke out in 1936. "The

Nazis consider this a dress rehearsal for the big war to come," he said. "That's why they support the insurrectionists with arms and planes and men. It's not just Spain that's involved but every last one of us."

But these words, like those of a few other farsighted individuals, were drowned in a sea of public apathy. Spain was soon lost to the side of dictatorship.

In the autumn of 1938 Sir Frederick, as chairman of the Medical Research Committee of the National Research Council, was asked by the Canadian government to set out on a coast-to-coast survey of the nation's medical research facilities. His 1935 report on Russia, which showed the democracies lagging behind in scientific matters, was thus bearing fruit after all.

For the next five months he traveled throughout Canada. He visited colleges and universities surveying research facilities. It was a tedious, wearying project. But he knew it was vital to Canada. Already the war clouds were darkening the skies over the free world. . .

During the endless train rides, Banting's one relaxation was sketching. He sketched everything and everybody. Once, while taking notes during a conference with a distinguished professor, he was caught in the act of caricaturing him on a page of his note pad.

"If I weren't sure those were notes, I would almost certainly think you were doing a sketch of me, Sir Frederick," the professor grinned. At the end of the discussion Banting autographed the caricature and presented it to his subject.

Another time, at a formal dinner in Edmonton, Banting was up to his old tricks of drawing sketches on the menu card. When the dinner was over, a charming young lady came up to him and presented him with a caricature of himself which she had done while he had been sketching the main speaker!

But aside from these brief moments of relaxation, the survey was hard work. It was completed early in 1939, and proved to be one of the most complete and significant studies of Canadian medical research facilities ever done. The findings formed the unifying basis for all wartime research activities in the Dominion of Canada in the field of medicine.

From the first, Banting knew the war to come would be won or lost in the air. Therefore one of his recommendations called for the organization of an associate committee on Aviation Medical Research. Such a committee was set up. It was under the National Research Council, and Banting was appointed its chairman. Throughout World War II the committee was to sponsor all work in the field of aviation medicine undertaken in Canada.

In the late spring of 1939 Banting took a few weeks off from his duties on behalf of the government. The reason was marriage—this time to Henrietta Ball. Miss Ball was a charming young lady who had worked at the Banting Institute in chemotherapy and tuberculosis research. Although the marriage had been planned for a number of months, only their immediate relatives and close friends knew the secret. The simple ceremony took place in Toronto on the second of June. Afterward Sir Frederick and Lady Banting left for a honeymoon up north on Lake Temogami.

They were back in Toronto at the end of August, and Banting plunged into work. But the happiness of the newlyweds was overshadowed by the ominous events abroad. The world was hovering precariously between peace and war, and each morning they scanned the newspaper headlines anxiously for word of last-minute peace negotiations. Banting tried to reassure his bride that there still was a slim chance for peace. But deep within he knew he did not really believe this.

On September 1, 1939, Sir Frederick Banting joined the Army for the second time in his life. It was nine days before Canada declared war. He told the lieutenant colonel who was the assistant district medical officer for Toronto, "I am going to war with you, and I don't give a hoot in a hailstorm what my rank or job is, just so long as I get into the thick of the fighting." He was immediately given the rank of major and assigned to work as a pathologist.

Soon Canadian government officials were faced with a curious dilemma. Sir Frederick Banting, discoverer of insulin and the nation's most famous scientist, was serving the defense effort in a dual role. He was a key figure in the campaign to mobilize science. But on the other hand, by having enlisted he was simply Major Banting attached to the No. 15 Canadian General Hospital Unit as a pathologist. Now a decision had to be made concerning which job would enable him to serve his country best.

To Banting's regret the government decided it would be a tragic loss to waste his research genius in an army hospital dressing wounds. Instead he was assigned a major organizing task. He was to set up and administer a large-scale research program and serve as liaison officer co-ordinating the work of British and Canadian scientists in wartime medical research.

Banting accepted the assignment, of course. He did not object even when he knew he would retain the rank of major, although his duties and responsibilities were the equivalent of a top-ranking general.

On the sixteenth of November he went overseas on a special mission. His job was to visit laboratories in Great Britain to learn all he could about the latest work being done there so he could bring the information back to Canada.

It was a grueling task that took many weeks. There was so much to find out and so little time in which to do it. He absorbed everything—new techniques, experiments with new drugs, advanced laboratory methods. But most of all he was interested in the problems of aviation medicine, the new branch of medicine dealing with man's physical and psychological behavior in flight.

In spite of the long wearying days, however, his thoughts turned often to Canada, and to his wife and eleven-year-old son. Early in January he sat down and wrote to young Bill:

My Dear Bill:

It is some time since I wrote to you and it is a much longer time since I heard from you. In fact I have not seen your handwriting since the last evening of spelling.

I hope you have done better in all your examinations this last time.

Well, your daddy has been very busy since coming here. I hoped that I would be on my way home before this but I really do not know when I will be home. When one is in the Army one has to do as one is told.

I hope you will act like a soldier, but I cannot hope that you will have to be one.

I hope you had a good Christmas and holiday—but

you will have almost forgotten about it by the time you get this letter.

Keep up your homework and be a good boy. I'll be home as soon as my duties will permit.

I hope you are looking after the snow shoveling and other things about the house. Carry on, Bill, while I am away.

Love,
Dad

Within a few weeks Banting was on his way home by ship. His head was buzzing with new ideas, and he was impatient to get started. When he arrived in Toronto he immediately ordered a decompression chamber to be built at the Banting Institute. This would enable investigators to observe the physiological changes that take place in the human body at high altitudes. It was the first chamber of its kind in Canada.

Decompression tests are always dangerous, so Banting insisted on being one of the first human guinea pigs. His colleagues advised against it, for he was now forty-eight and they felt it was a job for a much younger man. But Banting insisted and there was little they could do to dissuade him once he had made up his mind.

Time and again he entered the chamber and sucked in oxygen through a mask while the chamber was decompressed to simulate stratospheric conditions. During these experiments he experienced "the bends," a sickness that is caused by the formation of bubbles in the blood at high altitudes. But in spite of the excruciating pain, he insisted on going back in for more, for he knew that the knowledge thus gained would someday save the lives of youthful airmen.

One day he "went up" to forty thousand feet and stayed there for more than an hour! When he "descended" his colleagues congratulated him for setting a new altitude record. He now had the honor of being the first individual in Canada to be subjected to such a high altitude for such a long period of time.

However, not all of the flights took place on the ground. Banting knew that if the limitations of human endurance during flight could be licked, the Allied nations would be able to take a big step forward toward achieving supremacy in the air. And while decompression chamber experiments were valuable, such findings must ultimately be proved out under actual flying conditions if they were to have practical value.

Sir Frederick made arrangements with the Royal Canadian Air Force to go up in a speedy fighter plane piloted by a member of the R.C.A.F. The plane climbed, banked, looped and rolled with sickening repetition to give Banting a chance to study the effects of gravitational changes on the human body—his own. Finally, at his passenger's orders, the pilot dived the plane straight down at hundreds of miles an hour, then swooped up again suddenly so the scientist could observe how much a flier could stand before "blacking out."

In spite of his special interest in aviation medicine, Banting kept up to date on other important research projects at the institute. One of these was aimed at finding a method to neutralize the effects of mustard gas. One day his subordinates came up with what they hoped would be an effective antidote. They approached Banting for advice on how to test it.

"Test it on me," Banting replied calmly.

The researchers stared at him in disbelief, for they knew the danger involved if the antidote did not work as they hoped it would.

"No, I mean it," he insisted. "Apply mustard gas to my leg. When I feel it begin to take effect I'll use the antidote."

His assistants had long ago learned the futility of arguing with the "chief" once he made up his mind, so they did as directed. His leg was anointed with the blistering gas, and since it took some time for it to become effective, he took a supply of antidote home with him.

When Banting arrived at the house he noticed a trickle of smoke curling up from a corner of the garden. A brush fire! he thought as he dropped his brief case and raced into the house for a bucket of water. In the excitement the antidote slipped his mind. The brush fire was extinguished easily. Suddenly, however, he felt pain in his leg. He pulled up the trouser leg and discovered a deep mustard gas burn. The limb was badly swollen and required medical attention. "I want you to stay in bed for at least three or four days," the attending physician told him.

But Banting was up to his usual tricks. "I have too much work to do," he replied, "There'll be plenty of time to convalesce after we win the war."

The next morning, in spite of the severe pain, he forced himself to get out of bed, dressed and was off to the institute over Lady Banting's futile protests. The burn took six weeks to heal and left a deep, ugly scar.

Another task undertaken by the institute was to devise tests to enable the R.C.A.F. to select potential fliers more efficiently. Scores of young flying trainees were used to supply the statistical data needed for the tests.

One day a small group of future pilots wandered down

a hall in the imposing institute building, awed by the fact that they were in Canada's most famous research center. Finally, one of the young soldiers stopped a man dressed in an ancient short-sleeved laboratory jacket and tennis shoes. "Could you tell us where we can catch a glimpse of Sir Frederick himself?" he asked in a broad west country drawl. "It would be something to write home about."

The man in the tennis shoes grinned. "I don't know why anyone would want to 'catch a glimpse' of him, for he's not much to look at," he replied. "But for what it's worth you're looking at him right now."

The young westerner mumbled an apology, but Banting waved it away breezily. In a few moments he was chatting pleasantly with the group. By the time he said good-by to return to his office, the airmen were addressing him informally as "Sir Fred"!

Soon the experiments on high-speed and high-altitude flying began to show results. One of these experiments involved the use of mice in a swiftly whirling centrifuge. Banting's investigators found that when fluid was placed between the body of a mouse and the supporting structure, it acted as a protective system. The tiny animal was then able to survive an astonishing amount of gravitational force. It was an important discovery, and Banting and his researchers decided on a bold move: They would devise a flying suit containing a fluid to protect fliers against blacking out!

Within a short time a test suit was completed. Preliminary tests were undertaken in Canada and the results were excellent. The suit was then shipped to England where it was given further tests by a veteran Spitfire pilot under actual combat conditions.

The combat report was so encouraging that Banting immediately ordered an intensified program to improve the design so the equipment could be tested on a mass basis.

One afternoon Banting sat at his desk puffing on his pipe, reviewing the first year of wartime research. All in all, they were making good progress, he told himself. The hours were brutally long and the work was hard. But it was bringing results, and that was the important thing. Deep within he felt a glow of contentment, of inner peace . . .

• CHAPTER TWELVE •

A Healer Goes to Rest

In the summer of 1940 work at the institute proceeded at a furious pace. Banting's responsibilities were crushing. Yet for some strange reason he would often catch himself staring out the office window dreaming of his boyhood days. Perhaps it was the sweet smell of summer in the air or simply a means of escaping his burdensome duties for a few moments. In any case he found his thoughts turning once more to Alliston.

When their father died, brother Thompson had taken over the farm. Old Mrs. Banting, still vigorous in spite of her age, had been living in town until she had slipped and broken her hip. Now she was in the Alliston Hospital. Each week Sir Frederick sent her a fresh bouquet of flowers.

Young Bill was twelve. He was spending the summer on the farm. How Banting would have liked to be there now—to go fishing with him in the Boyne River and point out the secret places he had discovered as a boy. That reminded him to write to his son.

Dear Bill:

How are you getting along on the farm? I hope that you are a help to them now during their busy season.

You must work as much as you can, for in order to win the war Canada must supply England with food from the farms, as well as soldiers, planes and guns. So you see, by working you can help win the war.

I hope you have been in to visit your grandmother. . .

Be a good boy and do as you are told—and do not leave jobs half done.

Love,
Dad

The improved flying suits were ready early in 1941. In addition to the equipment, a great amount of research data had been compiled in Canadian laboratories since he had last been to England. Now he decided the time had come for another mission overseas to transmit these findings.

Banting decided to take along a young colleague Dr. W. F. Franks, who had been working with him on the flying suit project. It was agreed that Franks would travel by ship with the heavy suits while Sir Frederick would go by plane to allow more time for conferences with research officials in Great Britain. They were to meet in England.

Banting and his wife and son spent his last evening in Toronto visiting his cousin Dr. Fred Hipwell. They reminisced about their boyhood days in Alliston and the years together in medical school. He told Cousin Fred that someday, when the war was over, he would like to buy a farm near Thompson's. It would be a good thing for young Bill to be able to divide his time between the city and the healthy outdoors, he explained. Hipwell agreed it was a fine plan.

Toward the end of the evening Cousin Fred, who was an expert amateur photographer, took out his cameras and lights and insisted that the Bantings sit for pictures. Sir Frederick appeared gay and lighthearted during the photographing. But it seemed to Hipwell that his cousin was somewhat more tense than usual . . . that behind the smile was the trace of a shadow.

The next morning Banting was up early. Lady Banting, young Bill and David Howarth, a young war guest from England, came downstairs to join him for breakfast. Finally, he put on his overcoat kissed his wife good-by and shook hands with the two boys. As a last impulsive gesture he bent down and gave his son a hug. "You boys are the men of the house while I'm gone, so take good care of things," he told them. The door slammed quickly, and he was gone.

Banting proceeded to Montreal. He checked into a hotel and met with Dr. Collip, who had worked with him and Charles Best for a short time on the purification of insulin. Collip was now chairman of the Department of Medical Research at McGill University and chairman of an important committee of the National Research Council, and there were many vital official matters to discuss.

Finally Collip asked if he were dressed warmly enough for the plane trip. Sir Frederick admitted he had forgotten to bring along warm gloves. Collip lent him a pair lined with soft sheepskin. As Banting tucked them in his coat pocket Collip noticed he was wearing a funny little half-smile.

"You look as if you've just thought of a good joke," Collip observed.

"Not a joke," Banting replied, "but a curious feeling. I've had it since last night. Tell me, Bert, do you believe in presentiments?"

It was a strange question. Collip darted a glance at Sir Frederick. He was still wearing that tight little half-smile.

"I haven't thought much about it," Collip said trying to sound matter of fact. "Someday, I suppose, we'll find scientific evidence either for or against. As of now I can't say I feel strongly one way or the other. Why do you ask, Fred?"

"Because I have a funny feeling something is going to happen on this trip," Banting said.

Collip tried to reassure him. "Probably it's just overwork that's got you feeling like this," he said. "You've been driving yourself hard. You need a good rest. In fact it might be a good idea to postpone the trip for a few days."

"Nonsense," Banting retorted. "I'll be all right. I feel better already for having had this little chat." Nothing more was said about it.

It was a smooth flight from Montreal to the R.C.A.F. station at Gander, Newfoundland. Gander was the take-off point for wartime air travel over the Atlantic. The field was isolated in a desolate stretch of wild timberland and small lakes.

Even before the giant transport plane nosed down for its landing, Banting was already impatient to begin the long flight over the icy Atlantic. He half hoped the bomber in which he was to make the crossing would be waiting.

But when he reported to the headquarters building he learned the plane had not yet arrived, and he would have to stay at Gander for several days.

For the next three days he spent most of his time with Flying Officer Clifford Wilson, the chief medical officer. They discussed aviation medicine, the war and their future plans. Sir Frederick also took the opportunity to write Lady Banting a long letter. He sent his love to the boys and promised that he would return from Great Britain as soon as he could.

The day of departure dawned dull and gray. By late afternoon the wind was up and there were flurries of snow. Banting anxiously searched the sky a dozen times for the arrival of the plane. Finally, in early evening there was the unmistakable sound of motors in the distance. He raced out to the flight line to watch the approach of the ship as it roared in from the southwest. As it touched down on the long bleak runway he recognized it as a Lockheed Hudson twin-engine bomber.

A few minutes later Sir Frederick was introduced to the pilot. He was Captain Joseph Mackey, a thirty-three-year-old American and a civilian ferry pilot with the R.C.A.F. Mackey, who hailed from Kansas City, was a veteran flier with many years of experience as a test pilot and U.S. Army flying instructor. Banting also met Flying Officer William Bird, the navigator, and the radio operator Bill Snailham.

While the plane was being fueled and checked, Sir Frederick went to the hangar where the medical officer, Wilson, helped him into the cumbersome flying suit. Then they shook hands. "Wilson," Banting said half seriously, "I want to make a confession. I'm scared. I had a queer feeling the other night, but it went away. Now it's back again."

"It's a common enough feeling just before take-off," the medical officer assured him as he adjusted Sir Frederick's parachute harness. "You'll be all right, sir."

Banting lumbered across the flight apron in the clumsy suit toward the big Hudson. "Happy landings!" Wilson shouted.

The scientist waved and disappeared into the cabin of the plane.

Moments later the huge propellers bit into the cold Newfoundland air and the powerful engines came to life with a roar. The plane nosed across the field to the head of the runway. It paused while the pilot revved up his motors, then turned into the wind for the take-off.

The ship rolled down the strip slowly at first but soon picked up speed. There was a gentle lurch as the ground dropped away beneath them. The Hudson headed east.

It was evening now and snow was falling, falling softly on the dark, desolate land below. The night was a great fist closing in. They crossed the coast. The Atlantic Ocean was an endless pool of black. The engines droned on, trailed by the eerie tongues of blue exhaust flame.

Suddenly there was a sickening jolt as one of the motors began to gasp and sputter. In the cockpit up front Pilot Mackey cursed silently and checked his instruments. A moment later the engine died for good. Mackey feathered the prop and banked the ship around in a tight arc to head back toward Newfoundland. He jettisoned the main fuel cargo, then called through the intercom for the three men to throw overboard all the luggage and every item they could find to lighten the load.

While Mackey nursed the plane blindly through the night, the remaining engine coughed several times. Snailham radioed Gander that they had turned back. He asked for a bearing. It never came. "The receiver has gone out," he reported to the pilot.

Navigator Bird checked his charts and flight plan. His rough calculations showed they were over land. He asked Mackey for instructions.

"Bail out, everyone," the captain ordered. "I'm going to ride her down."

Back in the cabin, Banting, Bird and Snailham held a quick conference. To jump meant the risk of separation in subzero weather in the rugged wilderness. Moreover, Bird admitted there was no way of checking the position he estimated. They might still be over water. On the other hand, if Mackey were taking the ship down it meant he felt there was a fighting chance of landing safely. It was a life-and-death decision. Which was it to be?

A few moments were all they needed to make up their minds. They would ride the plane down and take potluck with Mackey!

Up front the pilot was waging a valiant fight to bring his injured ship down in the night's blackness. He was flying wholly by instruments, gambling that since most of Newfoundland was flat wasteland or frozen lakes he would be lucky enough to pancake in without striking any obstacles.

Mackey dropped full flaps and nosed the plane toward the ground. The altimeter indicated they were almost at ground level when he eased the stick back for the final stall.

The huge Hudson bomber struck down hard, one wing caught by a giant tree whose branches had reached out of the darkness. It plowed into the soft, powdery snow with tremendous force. Then it lay still, its metal body twisted, broken and helpless. The tragedy in the ghostly white expanse of frozen Newfoundland had taken place only twelve minutes from the time the plane had left Gander. . .

When Captain Mackey opened his eyes the cabin lights were still burning. His head was throbbing. He touched his fingers to his scalp and found he was bleeding profusely. He glanced at his watch. It showed he had been unconscious for a full hour!

He crawled painfully out of his seat and staggered back to the cabin. A horrible sight met his eyes. There were two dead bodies—Bird's and Snailham's. At first glance Sir

Frederick appeared to be dead, too. But then he stirred. Mackey knelt down to examine him. He was unconscious, suffering from a severe head wound. In addition his left arm was broken.

Mackey raised Banting to a sitting position and managed to drag him into a bunk. He covered the injured man with a silk parachute, then ripped another chute to make bandages and a sling for Banting's arm.

There was little else the pilot could do now but sit by the bunk and keep a long, lonely vigil. Throughout the night Sir Frederick was unconscious and delirious by turns. Once he awoke to semiconsciousness and ordered Mackey to take down dictation. The pilot tried to calm him, but the injured scientist began to shout in wild delirium. It was like a weird nightmare.

Finally, to quiet him Mackey took out a pencil and pad. Banting, feverish and unaware of what had happened, began to dictate rapidly. He poured out information on scientific and technical matters. He used many medical terms. To a trained ear it might have made sense. But to the pilot it sounded like gibberish. He wrote rapidly, desperately trying to take down Sir Frederick's words. His fear was that the statements might not be merely the ravings of a semiconscious man but of great importance to the scientific world.

In the end the attempt proved fruitless. He could not keep up with the dictation, and soon his numbed fingers refused to move across the pages of the pad. But he continued to give the illusion of writing in order to keep from agitating the injured man.

Banting continued to talk rapidly, driven by a sense of desperate urgency. There were times when his eyes closed and his head nodded wearily. But suddenly he would awake with a start. "Must get this down," he would mumble, ". . . must finish the job." Then he would start to dictate anew. It was as if the unconquerable determination and stubborn devotion to tasks that had marked his entire life were continuing to guide his actions even during these tragic moments.

Toward morning, however, he lapsed into fitful unconsciousness. Mackey used the opportunity to force his way out of the cabin door against the howling wind. The plane was cradled in huge drifts of snow. The savagely bitter cold seemed to hold the world in an icy grip. The pilot discovered that by some tragic twist of fate the wing had struck the only large tree in the entire area. Now they were marooned in an unbroken sea of deceptively beautiful snow.

Mackey staggered back into the plane, took off his gloves and breathed on his cold-stiffened fingers. Sir Frederick was still unconscious. Search planes, he guessed, were out in full force. But he knew, too, that the Hudson, three-quarters buried in a great white shroud of snow, would be hard to spot from the air. Unless he did something, and did it fast, help would come too late for the injured scientist.

Before long Banting began to stir again. He was shivering from cold and shock, and the pilot covered him with another fold of the parachute. "It's cold," Sir Frederick mumbled through chattering teeth. "But soon it will be spring and the farm will be green again . . ." He slipped back into unconsciousness.

Mackey was desperate. There was only one thing to do: get help. He struggled out of the cabin and fought his way through the huge drifts. After only twenty yards he was exhausted. It was obvious that to travel this way was sheer lunacy. So he returned to the plane. If only he had snowshoes!

Suddenly an inspired thought struck him. He crawled up to the pilot's seat and got out his map board. He cracked it lengthwise and used friction tape to rig up a primitive pair of tiny skis.

Outside the plane once more, he stumbled and floundered through the great banks of snow. About two miles from the ship he paused, breathless and bone tired. His eyelids were jeweled with tiny ice crystals which made it almost impossible to see where he was going. There wasn't a sign of civilization. He decided to head back to the broken bomber.

The trek back was easier, for he was able to follow his earlier tracks. Soon the fuselage loomed ahead. He drove himself on. Fifteen feet from the wreck he stopped short. Directly in front of him was a drift of dazzling snow. In it lay Sir Frederick. By some superhuman effort he had managed to drag himself off the bunk and out of the cabin into the desolate wastes of Newfoundland before collapsing.

Sir Frederick was dead.

For the next two days planes droned overhead. But none seemed to notice the figure of the lone survivor waving frantically from the white wasteland below. Mackey used everything he could find that would serve as a flare or signal, but it did no good.

On the third day the pilot prepared to make his way out on foot. He checked his tiny, homemade skis and packed some emergency rations. Then he decided he would wait a few more hours. . .

Just before noon, he left the cabin and scanned the dull gray sky without hope. He was about to go back into the fuselage when he heard the distant hum of motors. Soon a search plane came into view flying low. It passed directly overhead. He shouted and thrashed his arms. The ship passed on, the sound of the engines growing dimmer and dimmer. Suddenly as it neared the horizon he saw it wheel sharply and approach once more. It swooped very low over the wrecked Hudson and dropped a note.

Mackey retrieved the message and with trembling, frozen fingers he fumbled with it until it was unfolded. It read: "Bringing Help."

The search plane climbed in a great spiral to gain altitude, then it began to circle round and round to pinpoint the scene of the crash. In a short time the sky above was swarming with planes. Supplies came floating down by parachute—a sleeping bag, food, medical kits and tools.

All of a sudden it occurred to Mackey that no one but himself was aware of the tragedy that had taken place. He proceeded to tramp out huge fifty-foot letters in the snow. First he printed his own name, "Joe," to let the fliers know it was he who was alive. Then he added, "Three dead."

Since the planes were not equipped with skis, landing was impossible. But a sharp-eyed pilot in one of the ships spotted two trappers hauling a sled about two miles away. A message was dropped. The trappers immediately dumped their load of rabbits and rushed to the rescue.

On Sunday, February 23, 1941, the news had been released to a shocked world that Canada's most famous son was missing aboard a military plane. The hours that followed were marked by anxious waiting. In a million homes prayers were offered up for Sir Frederick's safety.

Then, on the afternoon of the following day, the Honorable J. L. Ralston, Canada's minister of national defense, announced to a stilled assemblage in the House of Commons that Sir Frederick Banting was no longer alive. An audible sigh of grief swept through the legislative halls.

Back in the desolate wastes of Newfoundland the two trappers reached Mackey. He was in bad shape, suffering from shock and loss of blood as a result of his head injury. They piled him on the sled and headed for Musgrave Harbor, the nearest settlement. On the way they passed a second rescue party that had set out from the village to bring back the frozen bodies of Banting, Snailham and Bird.

Later, a simple ten-minute funeral service was held in the settlement church. It was attended by all the residents. R.C.A.F. planes, equipped with skis, landed near by. The bodies, draped in Union Jacks, were taken from the church and borne to the waiting airplanes. A bugler solemnly blew "Last Post," and a small village band played a hymn and "God Save the King."

Three days later the entire area in and around Malton Airport in Toronto was cleared of visitors and placed under guard. Just after sunset, the eerie silence that pervaded the almost-deserted airfield was broken by the hum of an approaching plane. The eerie lights of the airport played strange patterns on the ice-covered adjacent fields.

A huge camouflaged bomber roared in from the east and touched down on the landing strip. It rolled up to the R.C.A.F. training station at the airfield. With only the plane's crew and a few high-ranking government officials present, the body of Sir Frederick was gently lowered from the plane and loaded into a waiting hearse. The vehicle then drove slowly through the military area as a line of soldiers posted along the road and at the gate came to rigid attention and saluted.

In Convocation Hall at the University of Toronto—where twenty-four years before he had received his medical degree—Sir Frederick Banting lay in state. All Canada was in mourning. So were millions of others throughout the civilized world. Thousands of visitors patiently lined up outside the great assembly hall to wait their turn to file past the casket. Many wept openly as they viewed the last remains of one of humanity's greatest benefactors.

The funeral service took place in the afternoon. Lady Banting insisted on a simple, modest service which she knew Sir Frederick would have preferred. But there were full military honors. The flag-draped coffin was carried out of the hall and laid on a caisson drawn by an armored car. The procession slowly made its way to the cemetery where another brief service was held as the casket was consigned to the earth. Three volleys were fired over the grave by a squad of soldiers. Then the thin, sad bugle notes of "Last Post" penetrated the cold winter air.

About the same time memorial services in Banting's honor were held in many other parts of the wartorn world. From every corner of the earth tributes and messages of condolence poured into Toronto. In the midst of history's most terrible orgy of death and destruction, people paused to pay homage to a healer. . .

In the years since Sir Frederick's death his name has become legend and his memory honored many times. At the University of Toronto where he did his great work in the service of humanity, a Banting Memorial Lectureship was established to provide for an annual lecture by a famous scientist. In Canada, a camp for diabetic children has been named for him, as well as an R.C.A.F. hospital at Gander, Newfoundland. In the United States a ship, the *Frederick Banting,* was christened in his honor by Lady Banting. A high school in his home town of Alliston, Ontario, bears his name. And of course the Banting Research Institute,

Canada's leading medical research center, today continues its great work in the interest of human welfare.

Yet memorials take many forms. Some are stone or gold or bronze. Others are institutional in nature, dedicated to carrying on in the spirit and tradition of those they honor. Banting's memory lives in these, of course. But of even greater significance is the fact that it is enshrined in the hearts of millions of men, women and children to whom he has given the gift of new life and hope. It is memorialized, too, in the spirit of other titans of healing, whose courage and devotion to their chosen work have been given new dimensions of meaning by his example.

In the final reckoning these are Sir Frederick Banting's most enduring monuments, his true guarantee of immortality.

Bibliography

Banting, F. G. and Best, C. H. "Internal Secretion of the Pancreas." *Journal of Laboratory & Clinical Medicine,* February, 1922.

Banting, F. G. "Pancreatic Extracts." *Journal of Laboratory & Clinical Medicine,* May, 1922.

Banting, F. G. "The Value of Insulin in the Treatment of Diabetes." *Proceedings of the Institute of Medicine, Chicago,* 1922-23.

Banting, F. G. "Insulin." *Journal of the Michigan Medical Society,* March, 1923.

Banting, F. G. and Best, C. H. "The Discovery and Preparation of Insulin." *University of Toronto Medical Journal,* February, 1924.

Banting, F. G. "Diabetes and Insulin." *Canadian Medical Association Journal,* March, 1926.

Banting, F. G. "With the Arctic Patrol." *Canadian Geographical Journal,* May, 1930.

Banting, F. G. "Medical Research." *New York State Journal of Medicine,* March 15, 1932.

Banting, F. G. "Science and the Soviet Union." *Canadian Business,* February, 1936.

Banting, F. G. "Silicosis Research." *Canadian Medical Association Journal,* September, 1936.

Best, C. H. "Reminiscences of the Researches Which Led to the Discovery of Insulin." *Canadian Medical Association Journal,* November, 1942.

Collip, J. B. "Recollections of Sir Frederick Banting." *Canadian Medical Association Journal,* November, 1942.

De Kruif, Paul. *Men Against Death.* New York: Harcourt, Brace and Company, 1932.

Irwin, D. "The Contribution of Sir Frederick Banting to Silicosis Research." *Canadian Medical Association Journal,* November, 1942.

Jackson, A. Y. *Banting as an Artist,* with a memoir by Frederick W. W. Hipwell. Toronto: The Ryerson Press, 1943.

Lucas, Colin C. "Chemical Examination of Royal Jelly." *Canadian Medical Association Journal,* November, 1942.

King, Earl J. "The Late Sir Frederick Banting." *The Lancet,* April 26, 1941.

Stevenson, Lloyd. *Sir Frederick Banting.* Toronto: The Ryerson Press, 1946.

A Record of Proceedings at the Opening of the Banting Institute, University of Toronto, 1930. Toronto: University of Toronto Press, 1931.

"Sir Frederick Banting, a biographical sketch." *The Canadian Press,* filed Toronto, December 6, 1934.

Index

About the Author

I. E. LEVINE is a native New Yorker. He graduated from DeWitt Clinton High School and enrolled at the City College of New York as a physics major. After working on the college newspaper for two years, he was convinced that he wanted to be a writer and changed his major to English and the social sciences. He received his degree, went to work in the public relations department at City College, and in 1954 was appointed to his present post of Director of Public Relations. He has written many articles for national magazines, is co-author of several adult books and well known for his biographies for young people. He and his family make their home in Kew Gardens Hills, Long Island.